Practical Action Publishing Ltd
27a Albert Street, Rugby, CV21 2SG, Warwickshire, UK
www.practicalactionpublishing.org

First published 1987\Digitised 2008

ISBN 10: 0 94668 879 6
ISBN 13: 9780946688791
ISBN Library Ebook: 9781780444314
Book DOI: http://dx.doi.org/10.3362/9781780444314

A catalogue record for this book is available from the British Library.

The authors, contributors and/or editors have asserted their rights under the Copyright Designs and Patents Act 1988 to be identified as authors of their respective contributions.

Since 1974, Practical Action Publishing has published and disseminated books and information in support of international development work throughout the world. Practical Action Publishing is a trading name of Practical Action Publishing Ltd (Company Reg. No. 1159018), the wholly owned publishing company of Practical Action. Practical Action Publishing trades only in support of its parent charity objectives and any profits are covenanted back to Practical Action (Charity Reg. No. 247257, Group VAT Registration No. 880 9924 76).

Cover photo: Mali. Workers placing window frames on block walls.

PREFACE

While the African Regional Organization for Standardization (ARSO), the Commonwealth Science Council (CSC) and the United Nations Centre for Human Settlements (Habitat), as well as several other agencies such as the International Organization of Standardization (ISO) and the United Nations Economic Commission for Africa (ECA), have identified the crucial need for standards and specifications in promoting wide adoption of local building materials in Africa, the solution to this problem seems rather complex and demands a creative approach. Ultimately, the promotion of standards for local building materials requires an extensive effort in international collaboration - co-operation between developing countries which lack the standards and developed countries which possess useful experience, and support from regional and international organizations with a specialized interest in the subject. It is against this background that the Workshop on Formulation of Standards and Specifications for Local Building Materials was conceived and that ARSO, CSC and UNCHS (Habitat), as a collaborative effort to assist African countries in the field of standards and specifications for local building materials, provided the necessary inputs for the operation of the Workshop.

This report demonstrates the extent of international concern for promotion of the local building materials industry in Africa. The report is supplementary to the initial report of the ARSO-CSC-UNCHS Workshop on Formulation of Standards and Specifications for Local Building Materials. It is a collection of the main background papers presented by some of the participating international agencies and thus reflects the different yet related interests which each agency has in the single task of formulating standards and specification for local building materials.

Contents

PART I

STANDARDS AND SPECIFICATIONS FOR SOIL BLOCKS, BURNT-CLAY
BRICKS, LIME, POZZOLANAS AND FIBRE-CONCRETE ROOFING
BY
UNITED NATIONS CENTRE FOR HUMAN SETTLEMENTS (HABITAT)

Contents

INTRODUCTION

1. Standards and specifications are the basic regulatory instruments for ensuring quality control for both raw materials and finished products in the building materials industry. As such, they provide indispensable guidance to producers, by specifying basic processes, test procedures, equipment and any related useful data that could lead to the production of an acceptable product. Standards and specifications can be incorporated in tender documents and contractual arrangements for construction, so that they are important instruments for settling any legal disputes that may arise as a result of shortcomings in construction. Finally, standards and specifications can promote the safe use of building materials in construction as well as promote the popular choice of a material on the market.

2. In most developing countries, there are hardly any standards and specifications available for a variety of local building materials. Sometimes standards are formulated but they are hardly ever adopted in practice. Because of this situation, most traditional materials, such as soil blocks, are produced with low quality and are generally unpopular. Relatively new local materials, such as pozzolanas and fibre-concrete roofing sheets or tiles, are produced without any standardized guidance to quality control or manufacturing techniques, so that there remains a constraint to the promotion of these materials on a wide scale.

3. Despite the general lack of standards for local building materials, a few countries have made the effort to arrive at some sound technical basis for the formulation of standards on local building materials. In some exceptional cases, such as in India, the formulated standards have actually become workable and have

1

had a noticeable impact on the building materials situation. The purpose of this report is to take account of these experiences and provide a state-of-the-art summary of standards and specifications which have been formulated for soil blocks, lime, pozzolanas, burnt-clay bricks and fibre-concrete roofing. Although the bulk of the report concerns standards for physical and chemical requirements of raw materials, test procedures for raw materials and finished products, and specifications for the use of the materials, the drafting of technical standards is only a minimal activity in the overall requirement for promoting standards. There is, in addition, a need for complementary activities to get the standards understood and used by a large number of producers and builders who may be illiterate and often operate in remote areas with no access to basic testing equipment. There is also a need for reformulation of local building codes and regulations with adequate reference to the newly established standards.

4. In building materials production, there is an interrelationship between standards formulation, technologies for production of the materials and actual use of the materials in construction. A discussion on standards formulation will not be complete without adequate reference to these complementary issues. For this reason, two other UNCHS publications, (a) The Use of Selected Indigenous Building Materials with Potential for Wide Application in Developing Countries and (b) The Reformulation of Building Acts, Regulations and Codes in African Countries, provide complementary information to this report.

2

I. SOIL CONSTRUCTION

A. Properties of soil and basic test procedures

5. Soil is a material with variable properties. It is the inherent properties of soil which determine the ultimate quality, durability and performance of the material in construction. A clear understanding of the characteristics of a selected soil group is, therefore, a prerequisite for establishing successful soil-construction practice. To a large extent, failures in earth construction and the general unpopularity of the material are the result of lack of understanding of the properties of soil or the lack of basic analysis of the material prior to use in construction.

6. Soil can be classified into six main groups, based on their texture or grain size:

Group	Range size in mm
Pebbles	200 - 20
Gravel	20 - 2
Coarse sand	2 - 0.2
Fine sand	0.2 - 0.02
Silt	0.02 - 0.002
Clay	0.002 - 0

The composition of a soil, in terms of the grain-size distribution, determines the plasticity, compactability and cohesion of the material, which, in turn, determine its fundamental structural properties. Typical particle-size distribution curves for soils, based on the above classifications, are given in figure 1. Soil classification can be simplified into three groups - (a) fine-grained soil, i.e., not less than 90 per cent of the soil should pass through a 2 mm sieve; (b) medium-grained soil, i.e, not less than 90 per cent of

3

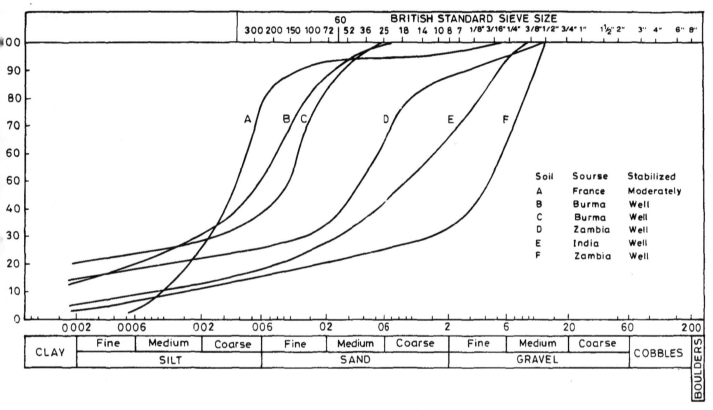

Fig.1   Particle-size distribution curves of soils

4

the soil, passes through a 20 mm sieve; (c) coarse-grained soil i.e, not less than 90 per cent passes through a 37.5 mm sieve.

7.   A simple field test can be undertaken to determine the particle-size composition of a particular soil and its suitability for production of stabilized-soil blocks. A sample of soil is placed in a glass jar, occupying one third of the jar's volume, and the jar is filled with water. The mixture is shaken vigorously until the soil is in suspension and, thereafter, allowed to settle for about half an hour. Normally, three distinct zones are observed and measured in the jar - namely, sand, clay and silt zones. The bottom coarse fraction should not be less than one third and not more than two thirds of the total settled mass. Where the coarse proportion is less than one third, some sand or other inert coarse material should be added. Similarly, where the coarse fraction is more than two thirds, some fine material, such as clay, should be added.

8.   In addition to the sedimentation test, other simple field tests can be undertaken to determine the suitability of soils for construction:

(a)   The smell test. The soil should be smelt soon after the sample has been collected. If the soil smells musty, it contains organic matter. This smell will become strong if the soil is heated or made wet. Generally, soils with organic matter should be avoided in construction.

(b)   The touch test. After removal of the largest grains, the soil is crumbled by rubbing the sample between the fingers and palm of the hand. A sandy soil should provide a rough feel and will not be cohesive when moist. A silty soil will give a slightly rough sensation with a moderately cohesive character when moistened. A clayey soil becomes plastic and sticky when moistened.

9. There are a few other tests which can be undertaken to determine the suitability of soils, but these require laboratory apparatus. The plastic index of a soil is normally determined, to give an indication of the tendency of the soil to swell when moistened and to shrink when dried. A high plastic index of a soil is generally an indicator that the soil has a great affinity for water and is not normally suitable for construction. The dry density of a soil is determined by drying a sample of soil at 105 ^{o}C and then weighing in a loosely filled container. Moisture content of a soil can be determined by measuring the loss in water from the soil sample after drying it at 105 ^{o}C. If the soil is to be used for stabilized-block production, water loss should not exceed 2 per cent.

10. The mineral content of soils, if established, can be a useful basis for determining suitability of soils. Soils with 15 per cent or less clay mineral are good for compressed-block production: soils containing expansive clays are to be avoided. Soils with organic matter exceeding 1 per cent, with sulphates greater than 1 per cent or with excessive mica flakes are also not suitable. Quartz and other siliceous minerals, limestone and marl are acceptable, but soils containing more than 50 per cent of iron oxides should be avoided or diluted with soils of low iron oxide content. Table 1 provides summary information on suitability of soils.

B. Soil stabilization

11. In soil construction, stabilization is only required where deficiencies have been determined in the functional properties of

the soil. Stabilization can take three basic forms: (a) mechanical, i.e., compaction of the soil resulting in changes in its density, mechanical strength, compressibility, permeability and porosity; (b) physical, i.e., the properties of the soil can be modified by acting on its texture - a controlled mixture of different grain fractions; (c) chemical, i.e., other materials or chemicals are added to the soil to modify its physical properties through a combination of physical and chemical reactions which occur between the soil grains and the chemicals, or to provide an impermeable layer or coating on the soil grains.

12.   There are four popular stabilizers for soil construction - fibre, cement, lime and bitumen. Fibre, as a stabilizer, hinders cracking, accelerates drying, decreases density and improves insulating properties of soil. The strength of fibre-stabilized soil blocks depends on the quantity of the fibres, but there is an optimum quantity which should not be exceeded. The minimum quantity for satisfactory results is around 4 per cent of the volume of the soil. The fibre should be chopped into pieces 4 to 6 cm long. Cement as a soil stabilizer has its greatest value when mixed with moist soil under compression. Plastic soils, in comparison with moist soils, require at least 50 per cent more cement to produce the same level of strength in soil-cement blocks. However, the highest compressive strength is obtained when soils with high fractions of gravel or sand, rather than silt or clay, are used. The proportion of cement required for soil-cement stabilization is normally 6 to 12 per cent. Certain additives, in small quantities, can improve the performance of cement-soil blocks - namely, lime (about 2 per cent) and soda-based additives (sodium hydroxide can be added in a proportion of 20 to 40 grams per litre of water used for the mixture). Lime

7

Table 1. Suitability of soils for use in construction

	Soil	Shrinkage and swelling	Sensitivity to frost action	Bulk density at O.M.C (kg/m3)	Voids ratio (vs = 2700 kg/cm3)	Compressive strength dry	General suitability (without stabilization)
GW	Clean gravel well graded	Almost none	Almost none	> 2000	< 0.35		Not suitable; fine soil should be added
GP	Clean gravel poorly graded	Almost none	Almost none	> 1840	< 0.45		Not suitable; fine soil should be added
GM	Silty gravel	Almost none	Slight to medium	> 1760	< 0.50		Suitable, but lacks cohesion. Erodes easily. Add fine soil
GC	Clayey gravel	Very slight	Slight to medium	> 1920	< 0.40		Suitable. Sometimes fine soils should be added
SW	Clean sand well graded	Almost none	Almost none	> 1920	< 0.40		Not suitable; fine soil should be added
SP	Clean sand poorly graded	Almost none	Almost none	> 1600	< 0.70		Not suitable; fine soil should be added
SM	Silty sand	Almost none	Slight to high	> 1600	< 0.70		Suitable, but lacks cohesion. Erodes easily. Add fine soil
SC	Clayey sand	Slight to medium	Slight to high	> 1700	< 0.60		Suitable. Sometimes fine soils should be added
CL	Low-plasticity clay	Medium to high	Slight to high	> 1520	< 0.80	Slight to high	Sometimes suitable. Sandy soil should be added
ML	Low-plasticity silt	Slight to high	Medium to very high	> 1600	< 0.70	Very slight	Suitable, but lacks cohesion
OL	Organic silt with low plasticity	Medium to high	Medium to high	> 1440	< 0.90		Not suitable. Sometimes acceptable
CH	Highly plastic clay	High	Very slight	> 1440	< 0.90	Medium to very high	Rarely suitable. Sandy soil should be added
MH	Highly plastic silt	High	Medium to high	> 1600	< 0.70	Very slight to medium	Very rarely suitable
OH	Highly plastic organic silt and clay	High	Very high	> 1600	< 0.70	Medium to high	Not suitable
PT	Peat and other highly organic soils	Very high	Slight				Suitable as sod

8

stabilization is similar to that of cement: non-hydraulic lime, either slaked lime or quicklime, is used. There are two basic classifications of bitumen - bitumen "emulsion" and bitumen "cut-back". Bitumen "cut-back" is not suitable for use in a rainy environment, and care must be taken to protect it from direct contact with fires because it is flammable. In preparing a stabilizer from bitumen "cut-back", kerosene is added to the bitumen in a ratio of about 1:4, and the mixture is heated to a temperature not exceeding 100 ^{o}C. Bitumen "emulsions" are, however, usually fluid and mix easily with soils which are moist. Bitumen "emulsions" can further be classified as: (a) anionic, i.e., not available on a wide geographic scale and not suitable for most soils, and (b) cationic, i.e., of wide occurrence and compatible with virtually all soils. In general, the use of bitumen in soil stabilization is enhanced by the presence of large quantities of water in the soil-bitumen mixtures. For this reason, the adobe technique of soil construction is the most suitable for bitumen stabilization. The quantity of bitumen recommended for mixing with soils in stabilization varies according to the properties of both the soil and the bitumen, but normally 2-3 per cent of bitumen is considered adequate.

C. Standards and specifications for stabilized-soil blocks

13. Stabilized-soil blocks of high strength, low water absorption and high durability require certain basic production practices, notably, a thorough mixing of the ingredients, avoidance of excess water, and good wet-curing of the blocks. It is important to carry out regular tests on samples of blocks from each production batch, to ensure the suitability of the blocks for use in construction. The following standard tests are recommended:

9

(a) Bulk density. A sample of the blocks is dried, and the weight is recorded. The weight is then divided by the volume, which gives the bulk density (kg/m^3): a high bulk density is an indication of high compressive strength. For each batch, an average of three blocks should be measured, and any block with a variation in weight exceeding 5 per cent should be rejected.

(b) Moisture content. At the time of use, the moisture content of the blocks should not be more than 4 per cent.

(c) Water absorption. A block is dried, and the weight is recorded as weight A. The block is then kept immersed in water for 24 hours, after which the weight is recorded as B. Water absorption percentage $= \dfrac{100\,(B-A)}{A}$. This test should be conducted on an average of three blocks, and the value recorded should not be more than 25 per cent.

(d) Shrinkage cracking. A sample of the blocks is observed for shrinkage cracks. Any block with more than three cracks should be rejected.

14. It is also important to determine the compressive strength of the blocks as well as the ability of the blocks to withstand variations between wet and dry conditions. For the compressive-strength test, a sample of three blocks, after each cycle of curing, is immersed in water for 24 hours. The adhering moisture is then wiped off the blocks, and the compressive strength is determined as in normal block-testing procedures. Any block with a compressive strength of plus or minus 15 per cent of average should be rejected, and corrective measures should be taken.

Normally, compressive strength of the water-saturated blocks, after 28 days at wet curing, should on the average be 2.1 Mpa. However, a strength of 1.4 Mpa should be adequate for a single-storey building. In undertaking the wetting and drying test, the following weights of a block sample are recorded:

(a) W_1 = The weight of a block after being cured and dried ready for use in construction;

(b) W_2 = The weight of the block after soaking it in water for 24 hours;

(c) W_3 = The weight of the block after drying in the sun after the 24-hour soaking in water ;

(d) W_4 = The weight of the sun-dried block after 20 strokes of a wire brush.

The process is repeated through six cycles, with each cycle representing an entire operation from W_1 through to W_4 . After this, the following statistics are determined:

$$\text{Weight of water absorbed} = W_2 - W_1$$

$$\text{Weight loss on drying} = W_2 - W_3$$

$$\text{Weight loss on brushing (abrasion)} = W_3 - W_4$$

$$\text{Porosity of the block/brick} = \frac{(W_2 - W_3) \times 100}{W_3}$$

$$\text{Percentage loss in weight per cycle} = \frac{(W_1 - W_4) \times 100}{W_1}$$

From the above analysis, a good block is one which shows no sign of erosion or flaking and having a weight loss of not more than 0.4 per cent after six cycles. A block should be rejected if it shows signs of erosion and breaks or disintegrates on handling.

15. Dimensions and weights of stablized-soil blocks tend to vary. However, two suitable standards can be specified:

    (a)   100 mm x 200 mm x 400 mm, weighing 12 kg;

    (b)   120 mm x 250 mm x 500 mm, weighing 22 kg.

II. BURNT-CLAY BRICKS

A. Tests on clays

16. Two sets of tests are carried out for quality control and standardization in the production of burnt-clay bricks. These are: (a) quality-control tests on brick-making clays; and (b) quality-control tests on burnt-clay bricks. Besides these two sets of tests, several standard specifications are required for brick-moulding plants, dryers and kilns, and codes of practice are required for brick-masonry operations and processes. Some of the tests described in the previous section for soil construction are equally applicable to burnt-clay bricks. For example, the determination of sand, silt and clay contents in soil by the sedimentation test, and determination of plastic and liquid limits and plastic index values are all relevant for brick-making clays.

17. In analysing the suitability of soils for burnt-clay bricks, information on the proportion of sand, silt and clay in the soil sample can be plotted on a triangular chart, as demonstrated with data on soils of India in figure 2. In general, loam and silty loam clays are suitable for burnt-clay bricks, and, similarly, soils containing clay, silt and sand in the following range are considered suitable for burnt-clay bricks:

Clay   :   20 - 30 per cent

Clay and silt :   40 - 65 per cent

Sand   :   Remainder.

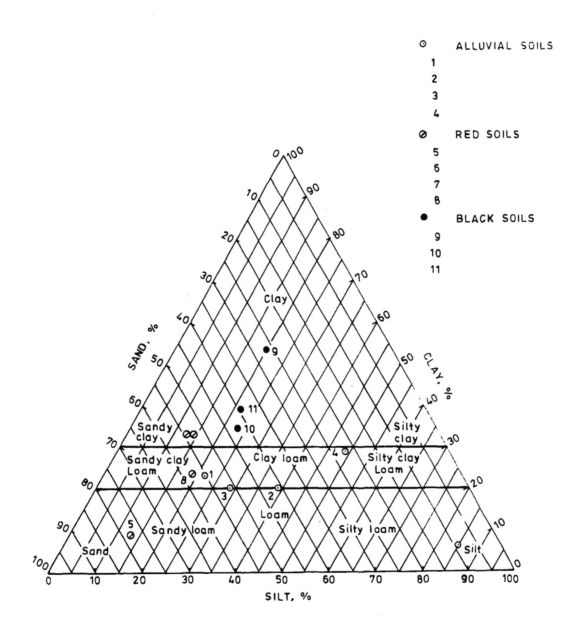

Fig. 2. Triangular diagram showing composition of soils.

Source: Rai, Mohamand Jai Singh, M.P. (1985) Advances in Building Materials and Construction 1st. edition.
(Central Building Research Institute, Rookee, India).

However, other types of clays can be made suitable for burnt-clay bricks, by either adding a plastic clay to a highly sandy clay or adding a non-plastic soil to a highly clayey soil.

18.   The suitability of clays for burnt-clay bricks can also be determined in well-equipped laboratories through:

(a)   An analysis of clays, to determine the percentage content of chemicals, such as carbonates, magnesium oxide, silica, alumina, and organic matter;

(b)   Determination of cation exchange capacity (T) - which is the maximum quantity of all types of cations that a soil is capable of retaining expressed in milli equivalents (meq) per 100 grams of soil; soils with a T higher than 80 meq are generally not suitable for construction, e.g., T is high for clayey and humus soils;

(c)   An X-ray diffraction test which is carried out by an X-ray diffractometer to determine the presence of clay minerals, such as kaolimite, montmorillonite, illite, mica minerals and iron minerals. Clays with a high content of kaolinite may require a high temperature of firing in kilns, whereas predominantly montmorillonite clays may require very careful drying and firing. The presence of iron compounds indicates that the bricks during firing are likely to get fused within a short range of the maximum firing temperature.

19.   The differential thermal analysis (DTA) is an important laboratory test, mainly for determination of the clay mineral content and the presence of organic matter, sulphides and carbonates. DTA gives a measure of energy changes which are due to the exothermic and endothermic chemical reactions of clay when heated gradually (about $10^{o}C$ per minute) up to to $1100^{o}C$. These

changes are recorded on a graph indicating exothermic and endothermic peaks. DTA requires a sample of about 0.5 g clay dried at 50° C. The clay particles may be pretreated by hydrogen peroxide, to remove the organic matter, before conducting DTA. In DTA, clays should be tested for percentage loss of weight in the following temperature ranges - below 100° C, 100° -150° C; 450° - 600° C and 800° -1000° C. The losses indicate the types of clay minerals present in the clay sample and their likely behaviour during moulding, drying and firing. However, the most valuable information about clay minerals is obtained by the exothermic peak in the DTA curves, particularly above 980° C where it indicates the presence of kaolinite clay mineral.

B. Field tests on clays

20. The composition of soils, in terms of suitability for burnt-clay bricks, can be determined in the field without any laboratory equipment in the following manner:

(a) The soil should be made free of hard stones, kankers, lumps of limestone and plant roots;

(b) The soil should be ground to a very fine state;

(c) A few kilograms of the ground soil should be taken and mixed thoroughly with water to the state suitable for moulding bricks;

(d) A few balls of about 6 cm diameter should be made and allowed to dry in the sun, and the soil may be considered suitable if there are no deformation or cracks in the dried balls;

(e) In case cracks appear, the soil should be mixed with sand in proportions of one-quarter, half and three-quarter parts of the soil, and the improved soil should again be formed into balls and dried in the sun.

The composition, after step (e), which does not deform or show excessive shrinkage and cracks will be suitable for burnt-clay bricks.

21. Simple field tests for determining the presence of chlorides and carbonates in clays can be undertaken with a small portable kiln containing a few glass test tubes, a spirit lamp, a few chemicals and a bottle of distilled water. The presence of chlorides can be tested by dissolving a small quantity of the soil in water and adding a solution of silver nitrate, with some nitric acid. A white precipitate indicates the presence of chlorides. Carbonates can also be tested by adding a little dilute hydrochloric acid to the soil. An intense effervescence, due to the generation of carbon dioxide, indicates the presence of carbonates. In general, clays containing carbonates are not suitable for burnt-clay bricks.

22. A moulding and drying test, for determining the suitability of soils for burnt-clay bricks, can be done in the field, using soil samples which show no deformation in their composition. The clay samples are prepared with different proportions of water and moulded in full-size moulds. After four days of drying in the sun, the moulded bricks should be examined at their edges and corners for deformation and cracks. The clay-water mixture which does not show any defect on drying is an indication of soil with suitable composition for burnt-clay bricks. An additional test to determine the correct plasticity of clay, based on the optimum soil-water ratio, can be performed by preparing a sample of hand-moulded lengths 3 mm thick, using various clay-water mixtures. The mixture that does not split on moulding gives an indication of the desirable water ratio.

C. Field tests on burnt-clay bricks

23.   A sample of bricks should be moulded from clays of varying soil compositions with varying water mixtures. These bricks should then be dried in the sun for about four days and fired in a small pottery-firing clamp. After firing, the bricks should be allowed to cool in the clamp and then examined for shape, deformation, cracks, colour and strength. The colour should be uniform and bright red. Two bricks should be hit against each other to assess the sound - a good ringing sound indicates good quality of the bricks. The water resistance of the brick-making soils as well as that of the burnt-clay bricks can be determined by fully immersing a sample of the burnt-clay bricks in a bucket of water for 24 hours.   If the bricks become soft, the product is unsatisfactory; hence, the soil has to be examined again, and corrective measures taken.

D. Laboratory tests on burnt-clay bricks

24.   For purposes of construction, a variety of burnt-clay bricks may be specified, namely, solid, perforated, cellular and special varieties.   The British Standard Specification BS 3921 part 2: 1969 gives testing methods for these varieties. Similarly, metric sizes for bricks have been proposed in the standards as shown in table 2. BS 3921 specifies a weight of 2 ton/m^3 for typical common bricks and 2.4 ton/m^3 for engineering bricks.   A minimum of 5.2 Mpa (5.2 Mn/m^2) is specified for compressive strength of solid bricks.

25.   The British Standards Specification does not specify water absorption, except for engineering bricks. A water absorption of less than 7 per cent by weight of the brick indicates high resistance to frost attack. The compressive strength of various

classes of bricks and the absorptive capacity of engineering
bricks, as per BS 3921, are given in table 3. Indian Standards
Specification IS: 1077-1976 gives compression-strength
requirements as shown in table 4. Good quality burnt-clay bricks
should not contain the following chemicals in excess of the
specified units:

(a)   Salts - 3 per cent;

(b)   Acid-soluble sulphates - 0.5 per cent;

(c)   Magnesium - 0.03 per cent;

(d)   Potassium - 0.03 per cent; and

(e)   Sodium - 0.03 per cent.

E. Remedies for lime-bursting, efflorescence and staining of
burnt-clay bricks

26.   The presence of limestone nodules in some clays is a common
cause of poor quality burnt-clay bricks. The size of limestone
(calcium carbonate) nodules has an important role in causing
lime-bursting. For example, one large lump of 12 mm diameter of
limestone in a burnt-clay brick can split the brick into several
pieces when it is in contact with water. Small pieces of

Table 2. Brick sizes

Co-ordinating size (mm)	Length (mm)	Width (mm)	Height (mm)
300 x 100 x 100	288	90	90
200 x 100 x 100	190	90	90
300 x 100 x 75	288	90	65
200 x 100 x 75	190	90	65

Table 3. Specifications for burnt-clay bricks (United Kingdom)

Designation	Class	Average compressive strength (Mpa)	Average absorption (percentage)
Engineering bricks	A	69	4.5
	B	48.5	7.0
Load-bearing bricks	15	103.5	Not specified
	10	69	
	7	48.5	
	5	34.5	
	4	27.5	
	3	20.5	
	2	14.0	
	1	7.0	

Table 4. Specifications for burnt-clay bricks (India)

Class	Range of compressive strength (in Mpa)		
350	35	–	40
300	30	–	35
250	25	–	30
200	20	–	25
175	17.5	–	20
150	15	–	17.5
125	12.5	–	15
100	10.0	–	12.5
75	7.5	–	10.0
50	5.0	–	7.5
35	3.5	–	5.0

limestone may cause only flaking of surface layers of the brick, although a large number of small pieces can make a brick swell up and soften. A 2 per cent content of 4.0 mm diameter limestone particles in a brick may cause bursting, whereas up to 5 per cent content of 0.5 mm diameter lime particles might cause no damage to the brick. One way to avoid the problem of lime-bursting is to grind finely the soils containing limestone particles before moulding the bricks.

27. In order to conserve energy, some inexpensive methods can be employed to tackle this problem. These are:

(a) The burnt-clay bricks are soaked with a sufficient quantity of water, soon after unloading from the kiln. In this way, any lime particles in the bricks will get hydrated without any expansion in the volume of the bricks. This process is termed "docking" of bricks.

(b) During the pugging of the clay, a quantity of sodium chloride is added - the equivalent of 0.5 to 0.75 per cent of the weight of the total amount of clay.

(c) An addition of 5 to 10 per cent of coal ash to the clay before moulding and firing of the bricks at a relatively low temperature of about 900 $^{\circ}$C leads to calcination of calcium carbonate particles within the brick. As a result, the particles of calcium carbonate are transformed into a porous structure of calcium oxide. When the bricks are wet, the pores within the calcium particles accommodate the expansion forces and thus prevent the bricks bursting.

(d) Soils containing limestone, if ground and passed through a sieve of 0.63 mm should be void of lime-bursting problems.

28. In burnt-clay brick construction, efflorescence seldom persists unless water is able to move through the bricks by capillary action and is driven out from a cool inner face to a hot outer surface. The remedy for efflorescence in brick construction is to provide a good damp-proof course at the plinth level of the wall. However, the addition of a small quantity of barium chloride in the clay and firing of the bricks at about 1050 $^{\circ}$C eliminate efflorescence to some extent. Where barium

chloride is expensive or not available, the alternative is to use sodium chloride up to 0.5 per cent by weight of the soil.

29. Some bricks show rust stains, owing to the presence of ferrous salts. The staining becomes prominent when the bricks are saturated with water, particularly on the mortar joints. It is recommended that the mortar joints be raked and left for six to eight weeks after construction, so that the stain develops on the raked mortar, and that the mortar be pointed thereafter. With time, the solubility of the iron salt in the bricks becomes negligible, and no further staining occurs.

III.   LIME

A. Standard classifications and basic properties

30. Comparable standards on basic properties of lime are provided in British Standards BS890, American Standards ASTM C110 and Indian Standards IS712-1973. In the Indian Standards, seven classifications of lime are defined as follows:

(a) Quicklime - a calcined material (mainly calcium oxide in natural association with a relatively small amount of magnesium oxide) which is capable of easy slaking with water (see table 5);

(b) Fat lime - lime which has a high calcium oxide content (and does not contain more than 5 per cent magnesium oxide) and is dependent, for setting and hardening, solely on the absorption of carbon dioxide from the atmosphere;

(c) Lump lime - quicklime in the form of lumps which come out of a kiln;

(d) Hydraulic lime - lime containing small quantities of silica, alumina and/or iron oxide which are in chemical combination with some of the calcium oxide content.

21

Table 5. Summary information on the chemical
requirements for quicklime

Constituents	Requirements (percentage value)				
	Class A (eminently hydraulic)	Class B (semi-hydraulic)	Class C (high calcium lime)	Class D (high magnesium lime)	Class E (Kankar lime)
1. Calcium and magnesium oxide					
Minimum	60	70	85	85	20
Maximum	70	–	–	–	75
2. Silica, alumina and ferric oxide					
Minimum	25	15	–	–	25
Maximum	–	–	–	–	75
3. Insoluble residue in hydrochloric acid	2	3	–	–	5
4. Insoluble matter in sodium carbonate solution	5	5	5	5	5
5. Magnesium oxide	5	5	5	not less than 15	5
6. Maximum loss on ignition	5	5	5	5	5
7. Carbon dioxide, maximum content	5	5	5	5	5

Note: In items 1 to 4, the values expressed are those obtained after
ignition.

(e) Dolomitic lime - lime in which the ratio of calcium oxide to magnesium oxide is about 55:45, the calcium oxide content is not less than 50 per cent, and the magnesium oxide content is more than 15 per cent;

(f) High magnesium lime - limes in which magnesium oxide is more than 5 per cent and less than 15 per cent and in which calcium oxide content is not less than 50 per cent;

(g) Hydrated lime - a dry powder obtained by treating quicklime with water, enough to satisfy its chemical affinity for water.

31. Hydraulic limes are capable of being used as a putty or mortar when mixed with water, and are also capable of setting and hardening when cured under water. Hydraulic limes are further subdivided into eminently hydraulic (class A) and semi-hydraulic (class B) limes. These limes are usually calcined at 1150° C to 1200° C, and the final product consists of calcium oxide, magnesium oxide and cementitious materials, such as dicalcium silicate and tetracalcium aluminate and ferrites. To a large extent, hydraulic lime is a mixture of lime and cement. The cementation value for class A and class B limes, as calculated by the formula:

$$\text{Cementation value} = \frac{2.8(SiO_2) + 1.1(A_2O) + 0.7(FeO)^{[1]}}{1.0\,(CaO) + 1.4\,(MgO)};$$

must be not less than 0.6 for class A lime and between 0.3 and 0.8 for class B lime. In table 6, detailed physical requirements for hydraulic lime (dry powder) are provided.

----

[1] Constituents (silica, alumina, ferric oxide, calcium oxide, and magnesium oxide) are expressed as percentage by weight.

B. Field tests for lime

32. The physical and chemical properties of lime, as described in tables 5 and 6, can only be determined in a well equipped laboratory. However, a few field tests as specified in Indian Standards IS. 1624-1974, can be performed to determine the suitability of lime for construction. Preferably, all the undermentioned tests should be conducted to determine the suitability of lime for use in construction.

33. In a visual examination test, lime should be examined for colour, namely, dirty white, white or pure white, and for the state of aggregation, namely, lumpy, powdery, soft or hard. High calcium lime (fat lime) should have a pure white colour. Lumpy and porous form may indicate quicklime. Dirty white colours indicate impurities in lime and, consequently, hydraulic limes.

34. The presence of carbonates in lime is determined by the hydrochloric acid test. A teaspoon full of powdered lime is taken in a test tube and tapped gently, and then 10 ml of hydrochloric acid (diluted with 50 per cent water) are added gradually. Excessive effervescence indicates considerable unburnt calcium carbonate or carbonate formed by long exposure of the lime to the atmosphere. The contents of the test tube should be shaken well and allowed to settle for 24 hours. The presence of carbonates is indicated by an inert material settling at the bottom of the test tube. From this observation, the purity of lime can be ascertained. For eminently hydraulic lime, the deposition in the test tube will show a thick gel and, for semi-hydraulic lime, a feeble gel. If there is no gel formation, the lime could be a high calcium or a high magnesium type.

35. The slaking characteristics of quicklime can be determined as follows: 1 kg of a lump of lime is placed in a bucket, and 3kg

Table 6. Physical requirements of hydraulic lime
(Indian Standards Specifications IS)

Characteristics	Class A, B and E	Class C and D
1. Fineness	Shall leave no residue on 2.36 mm IS sieve, not more than 15 per cent on 850 micron IS sieve, and not more 10 per cent on 300 micron IS sieve.	Shall leave no residue on 850 micron IS sieve, not more than 5 per cent on 300 micron IS sieve and not more than 10 per cent on 212 micron IS sieve.
2. Setting time	Initial set shall take place in not less than two hours and final set within 48 hours.	
3. Workability	-	Shall require not less than ten bumps to attain an average spread of 19 cm from an initial spread of 11 cm on a standard laboratory flow table.
4. Soundness	The Le'Chatelier moulds shall not exhibit more than 10 mm expansion	-
5. Compressive strength (minimum) for 1.3 lime-sand mix.	1.25 Mpa after 14 days and 1.75 Mpa after 28 days of water curing; in case of class A lime, the corresponding values shall be 1.75 Mpa and 2.8 Mpa respectively.	-
6. Transverse strength (maximum) for 1.3 lime-sand mix	0.7 Mpa at 28 days; for class A lime, 1.05 Mpa.	-
7. Volume yield	-	1.7 ml per gram
8. Popping and pitting (after steam treatment for three hours, using a set of samples made from 70 g lime, 10 g gypsum plaster and water)	-	Shall not exhibit disintegration, popping or pitting on the surface.

of water are added to it. If the lumps start crumbling to powder within five minutes, the lime is considered to be quick-slaking. In another bucket, 1 kg of lump lime is similarly treated with 1.5 kg water - if the crumbling of lumps starts within 5 to 30 minutes, the lime is medium-slaking, while a very slow-slaking lime is determined by the lump crumbling after 30 minutes. Alternatively, the slaking characteristics can be determined by inserting a thermometer in a bucket containing a sample of the lump of lime with a little quantity of water. With a high calcium quick-slaking lime, the temperature should rise to about 85 ^{o}C, and for medium or slow-slaking limes, much lower temperature than this should be observed. The slaking test is very important, as it gives a good idea about the quality and freshness of lime. A high magnesium lime is generally slow-slaking: eminently hydraulic limes and semi-hydraulic limes also show a slow-slaking tendency and a lower temperature rise than high calcium lime. Quick-slaking lime is preferred for building work, but slow-slaking hydraulic limes can also be used.

36. To determine the volume yield of lime, 1 kg of lump lime is crushed to 3 to 5 cm pieces and placed in a bucket. Thereafter, 600 ml of water are added, gradually stirring the contents in the bucket with a wooden rod. After the completion of slaking, the thick putty material so formed is transferred to a measuring flask. A quick-slaking, high calcium lime would show a volume yield of about two to three times that of dry lime. Low-volume yield may indicate that the lime is either hydraulic or a magnesium type. Normally, mortars, plasters and concrete ingredients are proportioned by volume, so that a high volume yield is an indication of high quality lime as well as of good plasticity and workability. High plasticity and workability properties are very desirable for mortars and plasters. The use

of lime, along with other ingredients for mortars and plasters, such as cement, pozzolana and sand, increases plasticity and workability.

37. To determine impurities in lime, the Indian Standard stipulates that a quantity of freshly burnt quicklime be slaked with a sufficient quantity of water in a bucket, stirred well and allowed to settle for two hours. The contents of the bucket should be transferred to a 250 micron sieve and washed thoroughly with water until the residue retained on the sieve becomes clean. After this, the residue should be fully dried and weighed. When the residue is up to 10 per cent, of the weight of the original mixture, the lime should be classified good, a residual value of 10 to 20 per cent indicates lime of a fair quality; a value above 20 per cent represents poor quality lime. However, this test is applicable only for high calcium and high magnesium limes.

38. The blotting-paper test for plasticity requires a sample of lime to be mixed with water to a thick cream-like consistency, left overnight and, then, spread in a thin layer over blotting paper. A comparison of the feel of plasticity with that of a standard quality lime can indicate the plasticity of the lime.

C. Workability test

39. To determine the workability of lime in a fied test is entirely a matter of judgement. The test is carried out on the same mortar mix as is intended to be used in actual construction work. By throwing with some effort, as for rough-cast work, a handful of the mortar on the surface on which it is to be used and by observing the area covered, the workability of lime mortar can be judged. The higher the area covered by the mortar, the better the workability.

40. Based on Indian Standard Specifications, the recommendations in table 7 are intended to provide guidance in the use of lime as

Table 7. Recommended mix compositions for commonly used lime mortars and plasters (Indian Standards.)

Type of lime	Mix proportion, by volume				Expected compressive strength at 28 days water curing (Mpa)
	Lime	Cement	Pozzolana	Sand	
1. High calcium slaked lime	1.25(1)	1	-	6	5.5
2. High calcium hydrated lime	2.50(2)	1	-	9	3
3. High magnesuim slaked lime	3.75(3)	1	-	12	2.5
	1.25(1)	-	2	2	2.5
	1.25(1)	-	1	2	1.0
4. High magnesium hydrated lime	1.25(1)	1	-.	6	4
	2.50(1)	1	-	9	3.5
5. Eminently hydraulic quick-lime	1.25	-	-	3	2.25
6. Semi-hydraulic quicklime or kankar lime	1.25(1)	-	-	3	1.75

Notes: Small quantities of lime may also be added to gypsum

mortars The figures in brackets represent the volume of

hydrated lime, whereas the preceding figure is the

equivalent for slaked lime putty. The quantity of

hydrated lime required to produce a unit volume of lime

putty is determined as follows:

$$Mh = \frac{G \times (Mp - 1000)}{G - 1}$$

where: Mh = mass of dry hydrated lime

G = specific gravity of dry hydrated lime

Mp = mass of lime putty.

a masonry material. Lime mortars can produce water-tight and durable masonry. However, the full strength development of lime mortars takes a long time. To overcome this deficiency, lime-pozzolana mortar compositions are being developed in which some accelerators, such as gypsum plaster, sulphates and carbonates, can be used in very small quantities to achieve early strength development. However, in disaster-prone areas, it is misleading to judge the suitability of lime as a masonry material solely on its favourable compressive strength. Here, the formulation of standards should aim at a material with other mechanical properties to resist forces of cyclones, earthquakes and similar pressures.

IV. POZZOLANAS

A. Clay pozzolana

41. The suitability of clays for use as a pozzolana can be determined by the differential thermal analysis (DTA) which has previously been referred to. In addition to this basic test, Indian Standards IS: 3182-1967 stipulates five other tests as described below. However, two of these tests - the reactivity test for both laboratory and field situations - are applicable to pozzolanas in general and not restricted to burnt-clay pozzolanas.

42. The clays for making pozzolana should be free from organic impurities, such as peat, wood, leaves, lumps and coarse gravel. The clays should have chemical compositions as given in table 8. A burnt-clay pozzolana should not contain any harmful impurities, such as iron pyrites, salts, coal, mica, shale or similar laminated materials in such a form as to affect the strength development when used in lime mortars. Indian Standards IS:2386 (Part 2-1963) stipulates that impurities should not be more than 5 per cent of the weight of burnt-clay pozzolana.

Table 8.   Specification for burnt-clay pozzolana chemical-composition (Indian Standards)

Constituent	Percentage of content, by weight
Silica, aluminium oxide and iron oxide	Not less than 70
Silica	Not less than 40
Calcium oxide	Not more than 10
Sulphur trioxide	Not more than 3
Sodium oxide + potassium oxide	Not more than 3
Water-soluble alkalis	Not more than 0.1
Water-soluble material	Not more than 1.0
Loss on ignition	Not more than 5

43. The particle-size grading of calcined-clay pozzolana or burnt-clay pozzolana for use in lime mortar should conform to the limits in table 9. If the grading of an otherwise suitable burnt-clay pozzolana falls outside this grading, it should be adjusted by grinding or screening.

Table 9. Requirements of grading for broken-brick
fine aggregates (Indian Standards)

IS sieve designation (IS: 460-1962)	Percentage passing (by weight)
4.75 mm	100
2.36 mm	90 - 100
1.18 mm	70 - 100
600 micron	40 - 100
300 micron	5 - 70
150 micron	0 - 15

44. A lime reactivity test is the main basis for considering the suitability of pozzolanas. The test, as per IS: 1727-1967, consists of making 5 cm cubes of a mixture of one part of dry-hydrated lime and two parts of a pozzolana at standard consistency. The cubes are allowed to cure in a water bath maintained at $50\,^{\circ}C$ for 10 days, and then compressive strengths are determined. If the average strength of six cubes is 4 Mpa or more, the pozzolana is considered to be suitable for use in lime-pozzolana mortar or in Portland-pozzolana cement.

45. A field test for determining reactivity of pozzolanas has been proposed by the Central Building Research Institute (CBRI), Roorkee, India. The method is based on the measurement of hydration properties of lime-pozzolana mixes. The sample of pozzolana under test is dried at about $110\,^{\circ}C$ for two hours on a hot plate heated by a portable gas burner. Then, 10 g of the

pozzolana are mixed thoroughly with 5 g of dry quicklime. The mixture is transferred to a 1 litre graduated glass cylinder containing 500 ml of water. The cylinder content is then shaken vigorously and allowed to settle for three hours. A similar mixture of the pozzolana and lime is shaken with 500 ml of water and then boiled in a flask on the hot plate for three hours while maintaining the level of water constant in the flask by adding hot water. The boiled mixture is then transferred to another 1 litre graduated glass cylinder and left to settle for three hours. After this, the volumes of the sediments in both cylinders are measured, and the difference recorded. These recorded values are then related to the corresponding lime reactivity values, as obtained from a standard graph (see figure 3). This figure shows lime reactivity against the difference in the sediments determined for a large number of lime-pozzolana mixtures. The above mentioned field test can be used in determining the lime reactivity of any type of pozzolana, but for each type a separate standard graph should be prepared.

B. Fly ash pozzolanas

46. For the purpose of determining the suitability of fly ash as a pozzolana, the specifications and tests are incorporated in Indian Standards IS: 3812 (Part I) 1966, as shown in table 10. Comparative chemical analyses of fly ash, from thermal power plants in India, the United Kingdom of Great Britain and Northern Ireland, and the United States of America are given in table 11. The mineralogical composition of fly ash varies according to the quality and fineness of the pulverized burnt coal, the type and amount of mineral matter associated with coal, the method of burning, and the control of the combustion processes. The mineral content influences the reactivity of fly ashes, and the

32

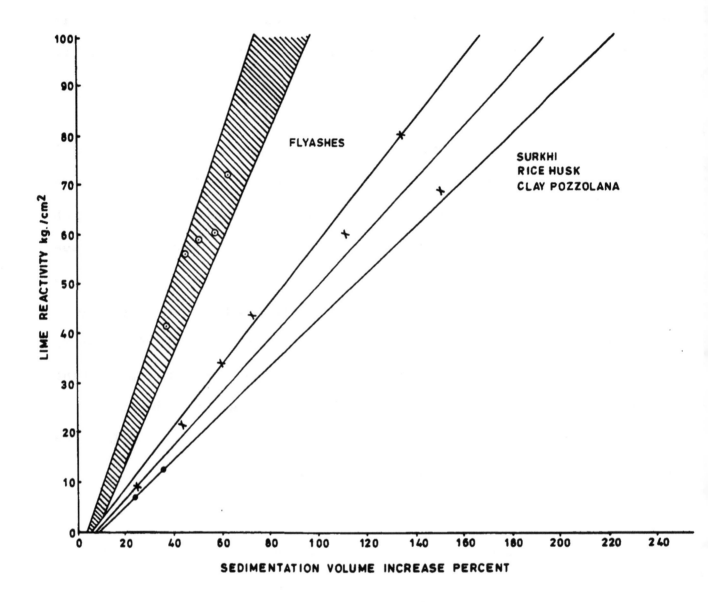

Fig. 3. Standard graph for determining lime-reactivity of pozzolana (a field test).

Source: Taneja, C.A. and Tehri S.P. <u>Accelerated field laboratory test for reactivity of pozzolana,</u>
N.B.O. Journal (India) vol. XXIV April 1979 page 2.

Table 10. Specification for fly ash for use as pozzolana, according to IS: 3812 (Part I) - 1966

Chemical composition (Percentage by weight)

(a) Silicon dioxide (SiO_2), aluminium oxide (Al_2O_3) and iron oxide (Fe_2O_3):	70.0 (minimum)
(b) Silicon dioxide (SiO_2):	35.0 (minimum)
(c) Magnesium oxide (MgO):	5.0 (minimum)
(d) Total sulphur as sulphur trioxide (SO_3):	3.0 (maximum)
(e) Available alkali, expressed as sodium dioxide (Na_2O):	1.5 (maximum)
(f) Loss on ignition, determined at 700° C	12.0 (maximum)

Physical properties

(a) Fineness: specific surface in cm^2/g (Blaine's method)	$3200\ cm^2$/g minimum
(b) Reactivity:	
(i) Lime-reactivity	4 Mpa minimum
(ii) Compressive strength (average) of 21 days water-cured cubes made of a mixture of four parts of ordinary Portland cement and one part of fly-ash by weight.	Not less than 80 per cent of the strength of the corresponding cement-sand mortar.
(iii) Drying shrinkage (percentage) of the test bars made of the same composition as for compressive strength test.	0.15 (maximum)
(iv) Soundness by autoclave test carried out on the same composition as for compressive strength (expansion after autoclave test is expressed as a percentage)	0.8 (maximum)

Mineralogical composition is determined by the X-ray diffraction

method. Generally, the higher the amount of glass content (non-crystalline phases), the better is the reactivity of the fly ash. Table 12 gives the general mineralogical compositions of fly ashes produced in India, Japan, the United Kingdom and the United States. Besides the minerals shown, calcite, siderite, pyrites, apatite and feldspars are found in very small quantities.

Table 11.   Average chemical compositions of fly ashes

Country	Constituents (percentage by weight)							
	Loss on Ignition	SiO_2	Al_2O_3	Fe_2O_3	CaO	MgO	Alkalines	SO_3
India	5.0	54.0	23.7	12.1	2.6	1.4	-	0.03
United States	1.2	47.4	18.2	19.2	7.0	1.1	4.0	2.8
United Kingdom	4.1	45.9	24.4	12.3	3.6	2.5	4.2	0.9

Table 12.   Mineralogical composition of fly ashes (percentage).

Mineral content	India	Japan	United Kingdom	United States
Quartz	5.0 to 12.0	5.4 to 11.8	1.0 to 6.5	0.0 to 4.0
Mullite	4.0 to 15.0	8.0 to 18.0	9.0 to 35.0	0.0 to 16.0
Magnetite	5.0 or less	-	5.0 or less	0.0 to 30.0
Haematite	2.0 to 5.0	0.5 to 5.3	5.0 or less	1.0 to 8.0
Glassy phases	60 to 90	70 to 85	50 to 90	50 to 90

47.   The loss-on-ignition value of a fly ash indicates its residual carbon content. Generally, the higher the efficiency of a thermal power station, the lower is the carbon content. Although a low carbon content is preferred for use of fly ash in mortar or concrete, a maximum of 12 per cent has been specified in the standard specifications of several countries. Fineness of

fly ash is also an important property for determining its suitability for use in construction. Fly ash with specific surface as high as 6000 cm^2/g is obtained in many thermal power stations, but, generally, values range between 2500 and 4000cm/g^2. Determination of specific surface by the Blaine's Air Permeability Method is influenced by the carbon content and also by the particle shape of the fly ash. No precise correlation has been found between specific surface and lime-reactivity values for fly ash, but fly ash with coarse particles or with specific surface below 2500 cm^2/g is considered unsuitable for use in construction. Usually, fly ash with a spherical particle shape is an indication of its suitability for use in construction.

C.   The use of fly ash in Portland-pozzolana cement

48.   Fly ash is extensively used in the manufacture of Portland-pozzolana cement by intergrinding or blending Portland cement and fly ash. Different countries permit the addition of different quantities of fly ash to Portland cement, but in general the proportion of fly ash ranges from 15 to 40 per cent. The main criterion is that the Portland-pozzolana cement (PPC) should be comparable in strength and related properties to ordinary Portland cement. The requirements for both types of cement as specified in Indian Standards IS:1489-1976 and IS: 269-1976 are given in table 13. In some countries, PPC is often not recommended for use in structural concrete, on account of occasional failures in meeting the standard specifications. Hence, stringent quality control in the selection of the pozzolana for making PPC is necessary. In India, PPC is specified for both unreinforced and steel-reinforced structural

Table 13. Specifications for Portland-pozzolana cement (PPC) and ordinary Portland cement (OPC) (Indian Standards)

	IS 1489-1976 (PPC)	IS 269-1976 (OPC)
Chemical composition		
(a) Loss on ignition (maximum percentage) determined at 1000 ^{o}C	5.0	5.0
(b) Magnesium oxide (maximum percentage)	6.0	6.0
(c) Sulphur trioxide (SO_3) maximum percentage		This value is not more than 2.75 when content of tricalcium aluminate is 7 per cent or less, but the value rises to 3.0 when the content of tricalcium aluminate increases beyond 7 per cent.
(d) Insoluble material, (maximum percentage) (i.e. where x is the declared percentage of pozzolana in the given Portland-pozzolana cement).	$\dfrac{2.0(100-x)}{100}$	2.0
Physical properties		
(a) Specific surface by (Blaine's method) (cm^2/g)	3,000	2,250
(b) Soundness:		
(i) Le Chatelier expansion test (mm)	10.0	10.0
(ii) Autoclave expansion test (mm)(maximum percentage)	0.8	0.8
(c) Setting times: Initial(minimum minutes)	30.0	30.0
Final: (maximum minutes)	600.0	600.0
(d) Comprehensive strength, MPa After 72 hours + one hour (minimum)	-	16.0
After 168 hours + two hours (minimum)	22.0	22.0
After 672 hours + four hours (minimum)	31.0	-
(e) Drying shrinkage (percentage)	0.15	-

concrete, and also for use in marine-atmosphere constructions, because of its sulphate resistance. Concrete containing fly ash as admixture gives low heat of hydration, making it highly suitable for use in mass concrete.

49.   These specifications are under constant review, as additional performance data are made available. For example, it may become necessary to specify stringent chemical requirement for fly ash with respect to alkali content, and strength requirements after three days curing for PPC. In fact, some other standards (for example, ASTM designation C595-68) have specified compressive strength requirements after three days' curing for PPC (see table 14). However, several grades of PPC are specified in some countries for use in mass concrete, ordinary plain concrete work and structural concrete, and in addition standard-quality fly ashes are bagged and supplied for various purposes.

50.   Fly ash is used both in cement fly ash sand mortar and lime fly ash mortar. Studies have been carried out to design mortar mixes, containing fly ashes equivalent to certain traditional mortar mixes, as shown in table 15. The strength and other properties of fly ash mortar are shown in table 16. The data for compressive strength, water retention capacity and drying shrinkage properties for fly ash mortars are based on experimental results from tests conducted in India. Standards on masonry mortars and plasters using fly ash are currently under preparation in India. In the absence of such standards and specifications, tests conducted so far have indicated that cement fly ash sand mortars produce higher compressive strength, higher water retention capacity and almost similar drying shrinkage properties to equivalent sand cement mixes.

Table 14. ASTM Designation C595 (American Standards) and IS: 1489 (Indian Standards) specifications for Portland-pozzolana cements.

		ASTM (American)		(Indian)
		Type P	Type PM	IS: 14
Compositional requirements				
(a)	Loss on ignition (maximum percentage)	5	5	5
(b)	Magnesium oxide, (maximum percentage)	5	5	6
Soundness				
(a)	Le Chatelier expansion (mm) (maximum)	Not specified		10
(b)	Autoclave expansion (mm) (maximum percentage)	0.2	0.2	–
Fineness				
	Blaine's method (m^2/kg) (maximum)	Not specified		300
Physical properties				
	Setting time, (Vicat)			
	Initial (minimum minutes)	45	45	30
	Final, (maximum minutes)	420	420	600
Compressive strength (Mpa)				
	3 days		12.4	–
	7 days	10.3	19.3	20.0
	28 days	20.7	24.1	31.0
	Drying-shrinkage maximum percentage	0.15	–	0.15

51. The average compressive strength and water retention values of lime fly ash mortars, as found in experiments carried out at CBRI are given in table 17. The strength given are considered adequate for brickwork, where the working stresses are not expected to exceed 0.45 Mpa. These mortars are, therefore, suitable for use in the construction of up to two-storey buildings, with a factor of safety ranging from 8.0 to 9.4. With

the inherent advantage of fly ash in terms of high-volume yield, laboratory tests have indicated that a fly ash concrete, using sands of fineness modules of 2.0 mm, provides a saving of 16.2 per cent to 20.9 per cent of cement, while sands of fineness 1.1 mm provide 19.6 to 22.1 per cent savings in cement.

Table 15.   Mix proportions of commonly used mortars and by volume (Indian Standards)

Cement sand mortars	Cement/fly ash/sand mortars
1:3 cement/sand	1:1.5:3 cement/fly ash/sand
1:4 cement/sand	1:2.0:4 cement/fly ash/sand
1:5 cement/sand	1:2.5:5.5 cement/fly ash/sand
1:6 cement/sand	1:3.0:6.5 cement/fly ash/sand
1:8 cement/sand	1:4.0:8.0 cement/fly ash/sand
Lime/pozzolana mortars	Lime/fly ash mortars
1:2 lime/clay pozzolana	1:2 lime/fly ash
1:3 lime/clay pozzolana	1:3 lime/fly ash
1:1:2 lime/clay pozzolana/sand	1:1:2 lime/fly ash/sand

Table 16.   Physical properties of fly ash sand mortars

Composition of the mortar		Average strength in Mpa			
(Cement/Fly ash/Sand)	Drying shrinkage (percentage)	Water retaining capacity (percentage)	3 days	7 days	28 days
1:0.0:3	0.104	11.2	3.1	5.6	12.9
1:1.5:3	0.114	17.8	3.2	6.8	14.4
1:0.0:4	0.106	9.9	1.7	3.9	7.4
1:2.0:4	0.112	9.9	1.95	5.8	8.0
1:0.0:5	0.106	6.5	1.2	2.6	4.1
1:0.0:6	0.98	1.2	0.9	1.6	2.5
1:3.0:6.5	0.091	15.3	1.0	2.4	3.9
1:0.0:8	0.093	-	0.9	0.9	1.3
1:4.0:8	0.088	16.3	0.47	1.77	2.2

Table 17. Compressive strength and water retention of lime/fly ash mortars

Mix composition (Lime/Fly ash/Sand (by volume)	Compressive strength at 28 days (Mpa)	Water retention percentage
1:2:0	2.39	70
1:3:0	2.72	68
1:1:2	1.05	65

Table 18. Properties of rice husk and rice-husk ash

(1)	Bulk density of rice husk	0.2g/cm
(2)	Chemical composition of rice husk	

(constituent)	Percentage by weight
Loss on ignition	18.7
Cellulose	42.6
Lignin	20.1
Pentosans	18.6

(3) Chemical analysis of rice-husk ash

SiO_2	13.20
Al_2O_3	0.59
Fe_2O_3	0.22
CaO	0.51
MgO	0.41
Na_2O	0.05
Loss on ignition	1.91

D. <u>Rice-husk ash pozzolana</u>

52. About 5 tons of rice husk. on complete incineration, produce 1 ton of rice-husk ash which contains about 90 per cent silica. Some basic properties of rice husk and its ash are given in table 18.

53. The pozzolanic property of rice-husk ash is derived from the predominantly non-crystalline nature of silica in the ash. The burning temperature plays a great role in retaining the non-crystalline form of silica in rice-husk ash. If the temperature of calcination of rice husk exceeds 700 $^{\circ}$C, the silica in the ash tends to transform into its crystalline form, such as the tridymite or cristobalite form, and the ash loses most of its reactivity, i.e., its ability to combine with lime in forming cementitious materials. As a building product, rice-husk ash is produced in the form of a lime/rice-husk ash binder ready to mix with sand and water for use as mortar.

E. Types of rice-husk ash binders

54. In rice mills, where boiling is carried out with steam before the husk is separated, rice husk may be used as fuel in the boilers. In this process, large quantities of rice-husk ash are generated. The ash is poorly crystalline and usually contains 5 to 10 per cent of unburnt material. This ash, when mixed with hydrated lime in the ratio of 2:1 by weight and ground in a ball mill to a fineness of about 4000-6000 cm^2/g, produces a lime-pozzolana mixture which can be used directly with water as a mortar or sometimes mixed with an equal volume of sand before use.

55. Rice husk and plastic clay can be mixed in a ratio of 1:1 by weight, using an appropriate quantity of water, and balls of about 80 mm diameter can be made manually out of this mixture. The balls are dried in the sun and then fired in a small trench kiln. The burnt material is ground to a specific surface of 6000 cm^2/g or more and, subsequently, mixed with hydrated lime in a ratio of 2:1. This lime-pozzolana mixture is normally used with two to three parts of sand for mortar work. In this process, no other form of energy is required, except the electrical energy

for grinding the balls and the energy used in the manufacture of lime.

56. Waste lime sludge obtained from the carbonation process in sugar or paper mills can be sun-dried and mixed with rice-husk ash in the ratio of 1:1 by weight. An appropriate quantity of water is added to this mixture from which balls are moulded. The balls are sun-dried and burnt in a small trench kiln, then finally ground in a ball mill to a specific surface of about 6000 cm^2/g. The lime-pozzolana thus produced can be used with one or two parts of sand by volume for mortar work. In this process, two waste materials are utilized, i.e., rice husk and lime sludge. Unlike the other processes in which hydrated lime is used, no energy is required in the lime used for this lime-pozzolana binder. The main drawback in this process is the unhydrated form of the lime sludge (CaO). Upon long storage (i.e., more than two months), the lime is likely to become hydrated and carbonated through the moisture and carbon dioxide of the air and thus lose some of the cementitious property of the mixture.

57. Rice husk can be burnt in a controlled condition in a specially designed furnace, to produce a white reactive ash for use as a pozzolana. The burning temperature is controlled between $600^\circ C$ and $700^\circ C$. The ash produced is ground in a ball mill, together with hydrated lime in the ratio of 2:1, to produce a lime-pozzolana binder which is used with two to three parts of sand in mortar work. This process requires more capital investment than the other processes, but any of the above mentioned processes could be applicable to the preparation of lime-pozzolana mixtures using the ash obtained from the incineration of other agricultural residues, notably bagasse, maize husk, coffee-seed husk or coconut pith.

F. Standard specifications for pozzolanas of plant ash

58. The statistics in table 19 indicate that the different types of ash obtained from the incineration of basic agricultural wastes have a similar chemical composition. For example, they all have high silica contents which, together with their non-crystalline nature, make them ideal pozzolanas.

59. Almost all the specifications and test methods previously identified for clay pozzolanas are applicable to the pozzolanas produced from incineration of plant wastes. Despite the similarities in a variety of pozzolanas and pozzolana binders, there still remain some differences which justify the need to focus attention on preparing separate standard specifications for each material. Such standard specifications should at least cover (a) methods of preparation of the binder, (b) chemical and physical properties of the pozzolana and the pozzolana binder, (c) methods of use, (d) curing conditions; and (e) storage.

Table 19. Chemical composition of pozzolanas from incineration of plant wastes

Constituents	Rice-husk ash (percentage by weight	Rice-straw ash (percentage by weight	Bagasse ash (percentage by weight
SiO_2	93.1	82.0	73.0
Al_2O_3	0.4	0.3	6.7
Fe_2O_3	0.2	0.3	6.3
CaO	0.4	1.5	2.8
MgO	0.4	1.8	3.2
Na_2O	0.1	5.3	1.1
K_2O	2.3	4.9	2.4
Loss on ignition	2.8	3.3	0.9

G. Lime-pozzolana mixtures

60. When specifying requirements for lime-pozzolana binders, emphasis should be placed on those issues which relate them to basic structural requirements in block or brick masonry. An example of this is found in Indian Standards IS: 4098-1967 which deals with lime-pozzolana. The physical requirements of lime-pozzolana specified by this standard are show in table 20. These specifications are based on high-calcium hydrated lime and highly reactive calcined-clay pozzolana and, therefore, may not be applicable for mixtures based on other types of cementitious materials.

H. Masonry cements

61. Masonry cements are finely ground mixtures of ordinary Portland cement and an inert material, such as limestone, slag or a siliceous material in a ratio of 1:1 plus a small amount of an air-entraining agent. These cements are marketed under certified specifications for masonry work. Currently, many industrial wastes are used for manufacturing masonry cements. Masonry cements are capable of achieving accelerated development of strength, owing to the presence of Portland cement, but, in addition, there are favourable properties of high workability and water retention, comparable to lime-based binders. Table 21 provides the requirements of physical properties of masonry cement as specified in IS: 3466-1967 and the ASTM Designation C-91. These are compared to specifications for ordinary Portland cement as contained in ASTM Designation C-10.

45

Table 20. Requirements of physical properties of lime pozzolana
mixtures; IS: 4098-1967

Requirements	Types of lime-pozzolana mixture		
	P40	P20	P7
(a) Free moisture (maximum percentage)	5	5	5
(b) Loss of ignition (maximum percentage)	20	20	20
(c) Fineness, percentage retained on 150 micron sieve	10	10	-
(d) Setting time, by Vicat apparatus			
(i) Initial (hours) minimum	2	2	2
(ii) Final (hours) maximum	24	36	36
(e) Compressive strength (average compressive strength of not less than three mortar cubes of size 50 mm composed of one part of lime-pozzolana mixture and three parts of sand by volume)			
(i) At 7 days (Mpa) minimum	2.0	1.0	0.3
(ii) At 28 days (Mpa) minimum	4.0	2.0	0.7
(f) Water retention (flow after suction of mortar composed of one part of lime-pozzolana and three parts of sand by volume minimum percentage of original flow)	70	70	70

Table 21. Requirements of physical properties of masonry cement and ordinary Portland cement

| Requirements | Masonry cements | | | Ordinary Portland cement |
| | IS: 3466 | ASTM- C91 | | |
		I	II	ASTM C-10
(a) Fineness on No. 325 (44 micron) sieve (maximum percentage)	-	15	15	-
(b) Specific surface, (cm^2/g)	5,000	-	-	6,000
(c) Soundness, auto-clave expansion (maximum percentage) (mm)	1.0	1.0	1.0	0.80
(d) Setting time, by Vicat apparatus.				
(i) Initial (hours) minimum	1.5	2.0	2.0	0.5
(ii) Final (hours) maximum	24.0	24.0	24.0	12.0
(e) Compressive strength, (average of minimum three composed of one part of masonry cement and three parts of graded sand, by volume)				
(i) At seven days (Mpa)	2.5	1.75	3.5	10.0
(ii) At 28 days (Mpa)	5.0	3.5	6.3	12.0
(f) Air content of mortar				
(i) Minimum percentage by volume	12.0	12.0	12.0	12.0
(ii) Maximum percentage by volume	-	24.0	24.0	-
(g) Water retention (flow after suction of the mortar prepared as for making cubes of compressive strength test-percentage)	70.0	70.0	70.0	-

V.   FIBRE-CONCRETE ROOFING (FCR)

A. Quality control of raw materials

62.   Ordinary Portland cement is the type used for FCR.   In order
to achieve the desired results in strength and durability, it is
essential that the quality of cement measures up to the standards
required for normal concrete and masonry practice.   Normally, any
type of sand which is suitable for cement mortars can be used for
FCR, but sand, despite being a relatively common material, should
not be taken for granted in terms of its quality and suitability
for FCR.   The size of sand particles has a direct influence on
the quality of FCR, and sands with particle sizes which will pass
through a sieve with 2 mm diameter holes but, at the same time,
be retained by a sieve with 0.06 mm holes are suitable.   The
absence of fine particles or the predominance of over-sized
particles leads to mortars which tend to split when the freshly
prepared concrete is being placed in the moulds.   Where the
mortar mix contains coarse particles of sand, the concrete may
become relatively strong after setting but will thereafter become
permeable.   Related to appropriate particle sizes, sand should be
well graded - that is, containing a good range of particle sizes
which upon consolidation compact to form a dense mass almost
without voids.   In addition, it is desirable that the shape of
sand particles be angular rather than rounded, so as to improve
the strength of the mortar.

63.   Fibres which are popularly used can be classified into three
main groups - mineral fibres, of which asbestos is the most
popular, animal fibres and vegetable fibres.   Vegetable fibres
are easily the most appropriate for the purpose of low-level
technology production of FCR.   The coir from coconut husk, stem
fibre such as jute, and leaf fibre such as sisal are the most
common examples of vegetable fibres which have been used with

48

success in FCR technology. In general, the selection of suitable fibres should aim at avoiding fibres with the following characteristics:

(a) Excessively stiff, oily or greasy;

(b) Easily impregnated by those chemicals which have adverse effects on cement, e.g. sugar;

(c) Susceptible to large dimensional changes from wet to dry state.

A simple test for suitability of fibres involves chopping up a sample of the fibre and mixing it in a sand-cement mortar of 100 times the weight of the fibre. The resulting concrete is allowed to set overnight. If the fibre pieces protruding from the concrete can be easily pulled out or if the concrete surrounding a particular location of fibre is discoloured or powdery, the fibre is unsuitable. The main function of fibre in the concrete is to resist segregation of the fresh mix during moulding and to prevent the formation of shrinkage cracks during the initial setting and curing stages.

64. Finally, the production of good quality FCR requires good quality water, preferably standard potable water. In most circumstances, rain water can be used, but, when it is collected from roofs, care should be taken to avoid those which are excessively contaminated with debris.

B.   Quality control in the production process

65. A basic check for quality production of FCR should take the following into account:

(a) Too much cement means unnecessary additional cost and it may imply an inadequate quantity of sand which leads to shrinkage cracks; too little cement and, therefore, excess sand may lead to a brittle and porous product. Cement-sand ratio of 1:1 or 1:2 is adequate for FCR sheets, while a ratio of 1:3 is recommended for

FCR tiles.

(b) Excessive quantities of fibre could lead to lumps, thus forming a porous and weak product: similarly, insufficient fibre leads to a fragile product, with little tensile strength, which may even break while separating from the mould. Normally, 1 per cent of the weight of the cement-sand mixture is accounted for by fibre.

(c) Excessive water will produce a deformed product, while too little water could cause unsatisfactory setting with traces of air bubbles in the undersurface of the finished product.

(d) Obtaining homogeneity, when mixing the fibre, sand, cement and water, improves the quality of the product.

(e) Good compaction of the fresh concrete mix ensures a product of the right thickness and improves durability of the product.

(f) Curing should not be taken for granted - bad curing practice could decrease the strength of the FCR product. One or two days' setting time under relatively humid conditions, rather than exposure of the fresh concrete to heat, plus seven days' curing in water, should be allowed.

C.   Strength and durability test

66. In undertaking strength tests for FCR, a distinction has to be made between two types of load to which the material will be subjected when used in construction. The first is the permanent or self-imposed load of FCR sheet or tile, which is a relatively high load, and the other the external load, referring to wind pressures and, possibly, the weight of people walking on the roof. Wind loads should not be underestimated - for example, a 140 km/h wind could result in an uplift pressure of as high as 90 kg/m^2, for which reason the strength of FCR products should be reasonably high to withstand such pressures. There are as yet no

standardized procedures to test the strength of FCR, except for adoption of standards for materials such as asbestos-cement sheets or concrete roofing tiles. For instance, the British Standards Specifications BS: 690 recommends a testing rate of about 1 per cent for a batch of asbestos-cement roofing sheets, and a similar standard is adopted for FCR: the age at which the strength of FCR products should be tested could also be taken to be two to three weeks. It is advisable to soak the sheets or tiles in water for 24 hours prior to strength tests, as recommended in comparable international standards for asbestos-cement roofing sheets.

67. A typical strength and durability test would consider the following:

(a) Impact test. This involves dropping a weight from a specific height, to determine the ability of the product to withstand cracking on impact of a load. When a 5 kg weight is dropped from a height of 1 metre on to an FCR sheet or tile, a good quality product should not crack.

(b) Bending tests. In order to determine the capacity of FCR to withstand bending stresses, loads should be placed centrally as line loads at the midspan of the FCR product. For a non-destructive test, a load of 50 kg to 100 kg, centrally placed, is adequate to determine strength for normal wind conditions. The load should be increased to 150 kg for hurricane conditions and to 200 kg for earthquake conditions. However, these have been considered too high and are probably only useful for conducting destructive tests. Another recommendation is that a central load of about 50 kg is adequate in most circumstances to test bending strength. Ultimately, popularly adopted standards will only emerge through a sustained period of field experience with the production and use of FCR.

(c) Porosity test. This is probably the single most important

51

test, because the function of a roof is basically to keep out the rain. In the absence of standardist procedures, international standards for porosity test on asbestos-cement roofing sheets, such as British Standard Specification BS 4624, have been recommended as a possible useful test on fibre-concrete roofing products. In this test, the sheet is laid flat and a head of water is maintained at 20 mm above the peak of the corrugations. After 24 hours, there may be dampness but a good-quality product should not have moisture on the underside. In general, the principle should ensure that a relatively large area of the sheet or tile is tested at a time.

D. A comparison between sheets and tiles

68. Table 22 summarizes the basic features of FCR tiles in comparison to FCR sheets. Sheets are normally supported on 75 x 50 mm purlins, spaced at 850 mm centres. Tiles rest on 50 x 25 mm battens at 400 mm centres. The volume of timber used is, therefore, less for tiles than for sheets. A 1 metre long sheet weighs approximately 20 kg, while a tile normally weighs 1.62 kg. For this reason, sheets are cumbersome and delicate to handle in the production process. The large size is a disadvantage in quality control for a small-scale manual production technology, and, similarly, it is a demanding task to lay the sheets over the roof. Also, the amount of cement per square metre of roof is greater in sheets than tiles by at least 30 per cent.

VI. A METHODOLOGY FOR STANDARDS FORMULATION FOR LOCAL BUILDING MATERIALS - THE INDIA MODEL

69. In most developing countries, there is an institution responsible for formulation of standards for a multitude of products. However, unlike other items, not very much has been achieved in the area of local building materials. In fact, in most instances, there are hardly any locally formulated or adopted standards, and, worse still, there is no effective methodological or institutional framework to respond to this need. Examples of countries with locally formulated and popularly adopted standards for a variety of local building materials are hard to find. India, perhaps, is an example where progress has been made in this direction, for which reason it may be worth reviewing the basic methodology adopted by the Indian Standards Institution.

Table 22. Summary of basic production data for comparison between FCR sheets and tiles

Product	Dimensions (mm)	Thickness (mm)	Effective cover (m^2)	Weight per m^2 (kg)	Cement content (kg)	Cement use per m^2 roof (kg)
Sheets	1000x780	10	0.62	32	9.0	15
Tiles	500x250	6	0.08	20	0.4	5

70. For the purposes of standards formulation, the Indian Standards Institute has a two-tier arrangement. First, there are divisional councils which are responsible for formulating guidelines and directives for a classified group of product: for instance, there are divisional councils for civil engineering, chemicals and forest products. The divisional council is made up of highly qualified professionals, i.e., scientists, engineers, manufacturers, economists and planners. Under each council,

several sectional committees are appointed to deal with specialized areas or topics. This is the main technical arm in standards formulation. For example, under the civil engineering divisional council, there will be a building lime sectional committee, a lime and pozzolana sectional committee, a bricks and soils building materials sectional committee and a sampling and quality control of building materials sectional committee. The divisional council may meet once or twice a year to review progress of work done by the sectional committees and provide directives for further work. Membership of the sectional committees is drawn from various research and users' organizations, and additional members may be co-opted from time to time as and when the need arises. Services to the sectional committee are, in principle, voluntary and not at any cost to the Standards Institution.

71. In most cases, for each standard, the technical content of the first draft is formulated by an expert from a research organization, a university, a practising firm or, even, a manufacturing company. The proposed standard is, then, discussed by the technical committee until a consensus is arrived at. The role of the representatives of the Standards Institution in the technical committees is mainly to co-ordinate activities. For this reason, any points of conflict in the committee, between manufacturers and users, is referred to a neutral body of scientists or researchers, a testing laboratory or, if possible, to another standards organization outside the country. For example, while discussing the first draft, a representative of the large-scale lime manufacturing sector may insist on specifying only machine-hydrated lime for use in construction, whereas a small-scale manufacturer may prefer the omission of machine hydration because it automatically disqualifies the products of the small-scale lime manufacturers from the market.

Such a conflict may be referred to a research organization, so that field samples from the two methods of hydration can be collected and analysed and the results and judgement submitted to the committee for guidance.

72.   After the first draft of the standard is prepared, it is circulated to other professionals outside the sectional committee for their views. For example, a draft standard specification for the design, installation and operation of a lime kiln may have to be circulated to, among others, members of sectional committees for steel, refractors, coal and air pollution, for them to testify the correctness of the grades of the various materials specified as inputs for the kiln. After receiving comments on the draft standard from a wide section of the industry, the committee discusses the draft with a view to arriving at a final standard. Thereafter, copies of the standard are dispatched to agencies or firms which may require them in their day-to-day operations. Sometimes, certain requirements of the standard may only be achievable in laboratory conditions so that they cannot be implemented in actual field practice, and, in such circumstances, provisions are made for a feedback to the Standards Institution for amendments to be prepared and issued separately.

73.   Besides standards incorporating specifications of materials and testing procedures, other standards are also formulated on quality control in the manufacturing process and on the practical use of the material. For example, there could be four sets of standards on burnt-clay bricks: (a) a standard specification for burnt-clay bricks; (b) a standard specification for testing methods on burnt-clay bricks; (c) a standard specification for sampling and quality control in the manufacture of burnt-clay bricks; and (d) a code of practice for use of burnt-clay bricks

in brick masonry. In the first two sets of standards, the properties of the bricks and testing methods are described, with relevant details of testing equipment. In the standard on sampling and quality control, details are given about the sampling procedures, and the number and quality of the samples to be drawn at each stage of the manufacturing process. In the codes of practice, details of use of the material for construction are provided, such as foundation details, quantities of brick and mortar mixes, with cross-reference to the respective standards of each material for the mortar, specifications about tools to be used, precautions and directions for laying of bricks, finishing and curing.

74. The certification mark scheme which is commonly used by several national standards organizations is also adopted by the Indian Standards Institution. It involves an agreement with the manufacturer to put a seal of the standards organization's quality-control mark on the material or its containers. An agreed fee for this service is paid by the manufacturer, and, if any lot of the product, on testing, does not conform to the relevant standard specification, it will have to be discarded or reprocessed. A quality-control mark is a legitimate guarantee of the quality of the material only in principle and may not necessarily be so in actual practice.

75. The time schedule for formulation of a standard could probably be specified, but the reasons for delays are difficult to analyse because of the multiplicity of activities involved. It is estimated that the time taken for the finalization of a standard is 36 to 40 months in Australia and the United States, while it takes about 52 months in India. One way to speed up the process of standards formulation is to generate a sense of urgency among manufacturers and users of a product for which

standards are to be formulated. Another way is to adopt a foreign standard as an emergency and amend it with time. Similarly, the standards organization itself can take the responsibility of formulating the first draft of the standard, in order to speed up the work of the technical committee. Invariably, each adopted standard should come up for reconsideration or revision after every five years.

PART II

METHODOLOGY IN STANDARDIZATION:

STANDARDS AND CODES OF PRACTICE FOR LOCAL BUILDING MATERIALS

BY

INTERNATIONAL ORGANIZATION FOR STANDARDIZATION (ISO)

CONTENTS

INTRODUCTION

76.   Ever since mankind first began to abandon his hunter-
gatherer way of life in favour of the settled existence of
agriculture and animal husbandry, he has been engaged knowingly
or unknowingly in standardization.   At first, he had to
determine, by trial and error, methods of constructing safe and
reasonably durable shelters from the materials locally available
to him.   However, once a successful design had been found, it
would have been quickly copied and elaborated on, and the
knowledge of how to construct such shelters would have been
passed from generation to generation by oral tradition.   Such
knowledge, although unwritten, can be considered to have
constituted the earliest building standards.

77.   These early shelters were no doubt constructed principally
from materials available in the biosphere (wood, animal hides
etc.), but, as small hamlets gave way to towns and cities, the
immediate environment would no longer have been able to provide
sufficient material for shelter for the increasing populations.
Hence, experimentation with stone, clay, earth etc. would have
led eventually to new designs, which would once more have been
rapidly copied and standardized.   This scenario, of replacement
of traditional building materials by others, would have been
repeated countless times over, so that, by the time of the advent
of writing, there must have been a great deal of knowledge of how
to construct buildings, which could be embodied in the first
written building regulations, standards and codes.   Indeed, as
long as 4,000 years ago, regulations existed in Babylon
concerning how to construct reliable and durable buildings.

78.   This historical perspective helps in formulating a general
definition of the term "building standards", which can be defined

as a "document describing a building material or product" or the method of using such a material or product in a particular application". This is, of course, a fairly arbitrary definition which, amongst other things, takes no account of the distinction between building regulations, standards and codes of practice. Nevertheless, it is useful in that it can help in understanding a second point, which is that building standards embody knowledge accumulated from experience and experimentation. Thirdly, it demonstrates that prehistoric and ancient builders were pragmatists: they would have had little knowledge of the chemical, physical and mechanical properties that make some materials more suitable for construction purposes than others. It was sufficient, in their eyes, to know that, if particular materials were used in a particular way, reliable and durable buildings could be constructed. All these points should be borne in mind, it is suggested, when considering the formulation of standards for local building materials.

I.   STANDARD SPECIFICATIONS FOR LOCAL BUILDING MATERIALS
79.   Two approaches, which can be called "descriptive" standardization and "scientific" standardization, are possible for the formulation of specifications for local building materials. If it is assumed that there is already a tradition in the use of materials in particular countries, the descriptive standardization approach will require nothing more than codifying existing knowledge. Thus, for example, for timber poles, it might be required that the wood be taken from a particular species of tree at a certain age, or when the trunk has attained a certain diameter, that it be cut to one of a series of standard lengths, and that it be seasoned, if at all, in a particular way. It might additionally be specified to what extent defects (for

example, damage caused by insects or knots) are acceptable for particular purposes and how poles should be marked or labelled to convey information to the user. In a similar way, a standard for bricks might specify their composition, dimensions, firing time, curing requirements etc. In such cases, a material or product is being described in terms of what it is. There is no question of trying to understand why the material is suitable for building purposes: its suitability has been proven in practice, and that is sufficient. It should be understood, however, that such standards will be very specific to the particular materials they represent.

80. Scientific standards, on the other hand, are not generally specific. They do not describe materials as such but, rather, specify the requirements they should fulfil. Hence, instead of specifying that wood should be taken from a particular species of tree when its diameter has attained a particular value, they would specify that, for example, the tensile strength should be not less than a particular value for a specific application. This allows great freedom in the choice of materials but it also implies a good deal of research into their properties, in order to be able to fix appropriate limiting values and to elaborate standard test methods to determine compliance with requirements identified by research. In turn, some method of representative sampling is necessary.

81. The approach to be adopted by developing countries in the formulation of standards for local building materials is, of course, entirely a question for each developing country to decide, bearing in mind the amount and sort of knowledge available and the extent to which facilities exist to undertake research in support of scientific standardization. It may be

that, in some countries, the descriptive approach should be adopted now but that a long-term plan should also be installed to replace such standards with "scientific" ones at a future date. In either case, it is suggested that standards should be elaborated according to a standard layout and should comprise at least the following elements:

(a) Scope - identifying the material and its intended use;

(b) Definition - of terms used in the standard which require explanation;

(c) Requirements - to be fulfilled by a material to ensure its fitness for a purpose (these may be in descriptive terms or in terms of the minimum properties that the material should possess);

(d) Sampling (in the case of scientific standards) - method by which some of the material (or product) can be taken for test purposes, with a reasonable expectation that it will be representative of all of the material (or product);

(e) Test methods (in the case of scientific standards) - by which the material can be tested for compliance with each and every one of the requirements;

(f) Marking or labelling - to inform the user about the material in question, such as its origin (as there will no doubt be differences in the "quality" of local building materials, even within the same country).

II.   CODES OF PRACTICE FOR THE USE OF LOCAL BUILDING MATERIALS

82.   No building material, no matter what its quality and suitability for a particular purpose, can guarantee in itself the construction of a reliable and durable building, if it is not used correctly and if workmanship on site is not of sufficient

quality. Hence, there is a need to elaborate codes of practice to provide guidance (or instruction) on the optimum use of materials. There will again be two possible approaches to elaborating such codes.

83. The descriptive approach will again require no more than observation of the tried and tested traditional methods of using the materials and the description of these methods to allow others to be able to repeat the process. This may include preparation of the site, transformation of the material, depending on the form in which it is supplied and in which it is used (for example, preparation of clay blocks from clay), together with the method of use and precautions to be taken during construction. Scientific codes of practice, on the other hand, because they are not material-specific, usually include items in the form of design guidelines. They assume that the user will be professionally qualified and experienced, and accordingly generally give recommendations as to 'good professional practice. The user is then free to adopt any procedures if he is sure that the results will be as reliable as those achieved when using the recommended procedures. Codes of practice can be developed for many applications, but, for those concerning the design of structures, ISO has provided guidance as to what they should contain in ISO Technical Report 8266 - "Guidelines for the presentation of International Standards dealing with the design of structures". One of the purposes of this Technical Report is to harmonize the presentation of codes for different materials (concrete, steel etc.), but it could equally be applied to local building materials and to facilitate harmonization of national and regional codes.

III. FINAL CONSIDERATIONS

84.   As mentioned above, there are two possible approaches to formulating standards and codes of practice for local building materials, and many factors will no doubt be involved in deciding which approach a developing country should adopt. Certainly, if it is intended simply to codify traditional usage and techniques, a descriptive approach would be the most economical in the first instance.   Nevertheless, it would be reasonable to expect that developing countries in future would wish to develop scientific standards and employ materials in new ways, particularly as, in the long run, they could have a potential for international trade, if only within one region.   This will inevitably, however, require a good deal of research into the properties of and techniques for using the materials.

85.   Building research and scientific standardization are resource-intensive activities, and one of the ways in which a country can make the best use of its resources is through international co-operation. One of the conclusions which emerged from the workshop organized in June 1986 by the ISO development committee (DEVCO), on the theme "Developing country needs in standards for low-cost housing", was that there was little that ISO could do to help developing countries to formulate the standards they require for local building materials and low-cost housing.   Existing ISO committees do not have the knowledge or expertise to be able to prepare building standards on behalf of developing countries, but the national standards bodies of developing countries are as much a part of ISO as are the European and North American member bodies.   ISO exists as a forum, where any member can propose to undertake work which is of mutual interest to several of its members.   So why should

65

there not be an ISO committee for local building materials, constituted by member bodies from developing countries, in which they can exchange information and experience and agree on basic standards which would help them to formulate their own national standards? There is certainly nothing in the ISO constitution or rules to preclude such a possibility. Furthermore, such an ISO committee could benefit from the collaboration established between ISO and international building research organizations - e.g., CIB (the International Council for Building Research, Studies and Documentation) and RILEM (the International Union of Testing and Research Laboratories for Materials and Structures), both of which are already involved in research into local building materials and low-cost housing.

86. One of the aims of international standardization is to facilitate the transfer of knowledge. Nowhere is it written, however, that such knowledge can only be transferred from developed to developing countries. The DEVCO workshop referred to earlier demonstrated that there is a need for developing countries to be able to exchange information on building materials and techniques amongst themselves, and an ISO committee would be an ideal forum for such an exchange. All that is required is that one member body be willing to take an active part in such a committee. The fact that 1987 has been designated International Year of Shelter for the Homeless demonstrates that lack of shelter is an international problem. It is one for which solutions should equally perhaps be sought internationally.

PART III

METHODOLOGY IN STANDARDIZATION

AND

FORMULATION AND APPLICATION OF CODES OF PRACTICE

BY

AFRICAN REGIONAL ORGANIZATION FOR STANDARDIZATION (ARSO)

CONTENTS	PAGE

67

INTRODUCTION

87. This paper presents the methods used to formulate standards
and specifications for local building materials and the necessary
steps required to be taken in respect of standardization
activitives. The paper is based on Ethiopian experience but
reflects the basic problems of standards for local building
materials in the African context, especially as they relate to
the present acute housing shortage. The first thing to be done
in tackling the housing problem is to exploit and develop the
available resources for building materials production in Africa,
but this can only be realized by providing at optimum cost the
necessary infrastructure that links sources of raw materials to
industrial production and construction sites. At the time of
identification of sources of local building materials, it is
necessary to undertake tests on samples in order to set quality
requirements. The development and formulation of standards for
local building materials thus become taxing, if accessibility to
raw materials remains a problem in African countries.

88. The African Regional Organization for Standardization (ARSO)
has given priority to developing and formulating standards for
local building materials. To this end, the ARSO Technical
Committee on Building and Civil Engineering (ARSO/TC 3) was
established to spearhead this particular task. The activities of
this ARSO/TC are described in the annex to this paper.

89. An African building code should unify the fundamental
approach to building regulations throughout the continent. This
can only become possible when the African countries work
together in this respect. It is also necessary to learn from the
experiences of other countries outside the continent, especially
those with similar climatic and economic conditions, i.e., India
with useful experience in the preparation of the Building Code of
India.

I. METHODOLOGY IN STANDARDIZATION

A. Characteristics of building materials

90. This paper focuses on local building materials, namely adobe, burnt-clay bricks, stabilized-soil blocks, lime, pozzolana and fibre-based roofing sheets. The main reason for focusing on these materials is that, if effectively developed, they would have a significant impact on the construction industry and, thus, improve the African economy.

91. Adobe is a Spanish word used for the building material made from sun-dried earth and straw. It is basically a calcareous, sandy clay, having good plastic qualities and drying to a hard uniform mass in arid and semi-arid climates. The usual method of making adobe bricks consists of wetting a quantity of suitable soil and allowing it to stand for a day or more to soften. A small quantity of straw or other fibrous materials is added, and the materials are mixed with a hoe or a similar tool. The mass is then trampled with bare feet. When it is brought to the proper consistency, the adobe is shaped into bricks in simple moulds. The bricks are allowed to dry partly while flat on the ground and are then stacked on edge to permit thorough and uniform drying. Adobe walls are normally built on a concrete base, otherwise the capillary action of groundwater may cause the lowest courses to disintegrate. The bricks are laid in a mortar of the same material, then finished with a coat of adobe, or, sometimes, with lime or cement plaster. With proper care in construction and maintenance, adobe proves durable. Its main advantages are its suitability in dry regions, its cheapness and its insulating properties. Its disadvantage is its weak resistance to wetting. The preparation of standards on adobe should be preceded by research into its characteristics and production methods, especially taking into account numerous

studies which have already been conducted in various countries. So far, there is no consolidated research work on adobe and consequently it is difficult to draw up standards at present.

92.   Burnt-clay bricks are usually made from red clay by burning different kinds of sandy soils: the soils for making bricks should contain less than 40 per cent silt (fine-grained sand). Bricks should be free from deep and extensive cracks, from damage to edges and corners and from expansive particles such as lime. They should be well burnt and have uniform colour and texture. Some African countries have national standards on burnt-clay bricks.   The most important characteristics to be considered are compressive strength, water absorption, efflorescence and dimensions.

93.   Stabilized-soil blocks are produced by a stabilization process which improves the characteristics of the soil. Soils used in the production of stabilized-soil blocks should not have less than 40 per cent of fine sand grains.   Normally, the stabilizing agents used are lime, cement and bituminous materials.   Cement builds up a rigid skeleton in the soil improving the quality of the material: lime reacts with the soil and changes its behaviour: bituminous material acts more or less as a water-proofing material. Stabilized-soil blocks can be produced in larger units than baked bricks, owing to the former having a low water content which minimizes the danger of shrinkage.   With a reasonable amount of a stabilizing agent, sand decreases the effect of shrinkage, thus reducing the risk of cracking, and also helps to achieve durability and strength. Not all soils are effective with stabilization.   The most important properties of soil for the manufacture of stabilized-soil blocks are:

(a) Particle-size distribution;

(b) Index of plasticity;

(c) Minimum water content.

Soils which are suitable for stabilization should be resistant to weathering when compacted.

94. Lime generally refers to the various chemical and physical forms of quicklime, hydrated lime and hydraulic lime. Lime can be used as a binder in the preparation of mortars and as a stabilizing agent. The most common raw material for producing lime is limestone. The limestone is burnt in a kiln at temperatures ranging from 900 to $1100°C$ to decompose the limestone ($CaCO_3$) into lime (quicklime) (CaO) and carbon dioxide (CO_2). Thereafter, burnt lime (quicklime) is allowed to cool and is put into a special type of tube mill, where it is crushed and ground to small grains. In order to obtain hydrated lime, the quickline is slaked with water, as illustrated below:

$$CaO + H_2O \underline{\hspace{4cm}} Ca(OH)_2 + heat$$

Where the limestone contains aluminia and silica (silicon dioxide), the decomposition process, after firing, leads to hydraulic lime, and the slaked product is known as hydrated hydraulic lime. In determining the acceptability, of lime, the main characteristics to be considered are chemical requirements, fineness, soundness, workability and compressive strength. Chemical parameters are expressed in terms of percentage of carbon dioxide, percentage of insoluble matter, percentage of magnesia and percentage of silica (SiO_2). Some National Standards Boards in Africa have national standards on lime which have become the bases for the formulation of Draft African Regional Standard Proposals 1/.

71

95. Pozzolanas are materials which, though not cementitious in themselves, contain constituents which combine with lime at ordinary temperatures in the presence of water to form stable insoluble compounds possessing cementing properties. There are two types of pozzolanas.

a) Natural pozzolanas, which are usually of volcanic origin;

b) Artificial pozzolanas, such as materials produced by heat treatment of clays, shales and pulverized fuel ash (fly ash).

Pozzolanas can be used as a replacement for up to 25 per cent Portland cement to produce Portland-pozzolana cement.

Portland-pozzolana cement can be used in:

a) Concrete structures which are exposed to attack by sea water;

b) Mass concrete constructions where pozzolanic constituents of the cement reduce the heat of hydration in concrete;

c) Construction which requires lower co-efficient of permeability to prevent expansion and cracking caused by reaction of the reactive silica contained in certain aggregates.

Portland-pozzolana cement also increases the tensile strength of mortars, but in general, the strength of the product is developed slowly compared with ordinary Portland cement. National standards concerning Portland-pozzolana cement and pozzolanas for use with lime are available in different countries. Ethiopia, as the secretariat of ARSO/TC3, has prepared Draft African Regional Standards Proposals concerning pozzolanas. 1/

96. Fibre-based roofing sheets is the term applied to a variety of roofing sheets made from different fibres such as asbestos and natural fibres. They are all characterized by their lightness and good sound and thermal insulation abilities, and

----

1/ See minutes of ARSO/TC3 meeting, Nairobi, March 1987.

they are usually cheaper than other roofing materials, such as
corrugated steel sheets. Draft African Regional Standards
Proposals have been prepared on asbestos-cement roofing sheets,
but owing to the inappropriateness and scarcity of asbestos,
other cheap fibres are being studied as substitutes for asbestos.
These studies focus mainly on natural fibres, such as sisal, jute
and coir. So far, results have not shown good flexural and other
mechanical properties of natural-fibre concrete roofing, but,
its ductility and impact-resistance properties are quite
acceptable. There is, however, hope of improving the weak
properties and popularizing the materials use for roofing.

B. Test methods

97. Building materials should conform to standard test
procedures. Standard test procedures (methods of test) can be
chosen from either ISO standards or other foreign standards after
considering a number of interplaying factors.

98. There are no standardized test methods for adobe. The
acceptability of adobe blocks can be determined by investigating
the durability and strength of adobe under different climatic
conditions and working out a systematic test procedure to
establish the quality. The method of testing burnt- clay-bricks
could help in drawing up the standard. A number of foreign
national standards for lime are available. The Draft African
Standards Proposals also include different methods of testing
lime. Some countries already have standards for testing
pozzolanas, and these standards closely resemble standards for
testing lime. There are no national standards for testing fibre-
based roofing sheets made of natural fibres, such as sisal.
Standards on test methods have to be developed gradually.

99.   The development and formulation of standards on building materials should be backed by research. It is also necessary to gather local technical information, if there is any, and compare this with the requirements of foreign national and/or international standards.   Draft proposals should be submitted to a review group, with members drawn from ministries, governmental and private organizations, research institutions and others agencies knowledgeable in standardization matters.   The approved draft standard proposals can then be distributed to the public for comments and amended in accordance with comments received. After this, the draft standards can be submitted to the legislative authority for final approval and subsequent publication.

100.   Developing standards on locally manufactured products is sometimes difficult.   The standards should reflect local conditions, and in order for this to be done, data must be collected. For this reason, the secretariat for ARSO on building materials tries to compile data from member countries.   Products which are peculiar to African countries and for which technical information as to their characteristics is not available require in-depth test analysis.   This exercise is demanding, because much of the work is dependent on the availability of testing facilities which most African countries lack.   Efficient standardization work requires qualified personnel, and, unless remunerations are competitive, it may not be easy to attract the desired calibre of staff for the task.   Normally there is a lack of manpower to undertake standardization work at both national and international levels.

II.   FORMULATION AND APPLICATION OF CODES OF PRACTICE

A.   Formulation of codes of practice

101.   A code of practice basically is an authoritative guide to the best accepted practice for engineering and construction techniques and for such wide-ranging operations as installation, maintenance and treatment of materials and provision of services. ARSO/TC3/SC2 is responsible for promoting codes of practice. The subcommittee has started its work by giving utmost importance to housing and related subjects.

102.   The principle for formulating codes of practice should be much the same as for formulation of standards for building materials. First, existing practices should be studied in order to identify good practices. Then, data from foreign practices, preferably practices under similar conditions, should be gathered and studied. Thirdly governmental and private organizations, which are concerned with codes of practice, should be consulted. After these processes, the secretariat can proceed to draft the codes of practice. However, in reality, codes of practice for construction methods using local building materials are yet to be formulated. The process of formulating codes of practice may be summarized as follows:

a) Choose that segment of construction that needs to be given priority;

b) Study various practices of that segment;

c) Analyse advantages and disadvantages and choose the practices that best suit the region;

d) Discuss with regulatory agencies and seek their approval;

e) Make sure the practices have statutory status so that they are easily enforcable.

B. Application of codes of practice in the use of local building materials.

103. The drafting of codes of practice is facilitated with the availability of standards on building materials. Codes of practice should allow the maximum utilization of locally available materials. There is a sound basis for formulating codes of practice covering the use of adobe, stabilized-soil blocks, burnt-clay bricks, lime, pozzolanas and fibre-concrete roofing, especially considering the wide range of experience both in the African region and outside it.

104. Perhaps lime offers the best opportunity for the formulation of codes of practice to promote the adoption of a local building material in construction. For one reason, there are several national standards for lime in Africa, so that it becomes easy to prepare codes of practice that allow maximum use of lime. However, it is important to prepare a code of practice that ensures wide scope for application of lime in construction. A draft African Regional Standard Proposal on Pozzolana has been submitted to ARSO/TC3, and it would be possible to use it in formulating codes of practice on the production and use of pozzolanas.

III. CONCLUSION

105. The development of local building materials and their use for the construction of low cost houses has been the theme of discussions at many national and international meetings. So far, very little has been achieved in the research activities aimed at overcoming the dependency on imported building materials: hence, effort should aim at strengthening capacities for research activities on locally available materials. The promotion of import-substitution strategy in this sector will undoubtedly make Africa self-reliant: however, this strategy

76

should be implemented cautiously in order not to endanger the national economies of African countries.

IV. BIBLIOGRAPHY.

1. National building code of India - 1970.

2. Guide for the formulation of Ethiopian Standards - 1976.

3. Roofing sheet made of mortar reinforced with natural fibres - by Zawde Berhane, 1986.

4. Some experiments on stabilized-soil blocks - by L. Holmgren, 1964

5. Quality of clay bricks and concrete hollow blocks produced in Ethiopia - by U. A. Halvorsen, 1968.

6. Preliminary investigation results on the pozzolanic properties of local scoria - by Zawde Berhane, 1987.

7. Explanatory notes on the Ethiopian Standard on lime.

8. Explanatory notes on the Ethiopian Standard on bricks.

9. Paper presented at ISO/SIDA seminar on standardization - by Yohannes Olana, February 1986.

10. Indigenous African architecture - by Rene Gardi, 1973.

Annex

ACTIVITIES OF ARSO TECHNICAL COMMITTEE ON BUILDING AND CIVIL
ENGINEERING (ARSO/TC3)

107.   ARSO/TC3 was established in 1981.   Its main objectives are
standardization of building materials in the African region and
development of building codes applicable to Africa.   It held its
first meeting in Nairobi, Kenya, from 20 to 25 October 1983.   At
that meeting, the creation of two subcommittees, i.e., the sub
committee for building materials (SC1) and the sub-committee for
codes of practice (SC2) was recommended. The responsibility of
ARSO/TC3/SC1 is to promote standardization of building materials
and components in accordance with the interests of the continent.
Priority is given to ISO standards to be adopted as African
Regional Standards.

108.   The first set of international standards on Modular Co-
ordination and Technical Drawings was introduced by the
secretariat at the first meeting of TC3 and was adopted as Draft
African Regional Standards upon considering regional conditions.
Timber being the main export item for Africa, TC3 recommended the
formulation of standards on timber and timber products, and
consequently the secretariat presented 12 ISO standards on
plywood and veneer plywood at the second meeting of TC3 which was
held from 23 to 26 November 1984 in Nairobi.   TC3 also directed
SC1 to formulate Draft African Regional Standard Proposals
(DRSPs) on cement, sawn timber and wood, including veneer
plywood, and also advised the secretariat on classification of
building materials and components used in building construction.
Accordingly, the secretariat prepared a report on classification
of building materials and components which was submitted to the
ARSO Secretariat in August 1985.   In addition to this, 14 Draft
African Regional Standard Proposals for Low-cost Housing were

submitted. The secretariat studied further ISO standards on timber, wood and veneer plywood, and recommended a total of 26 ISO standards for adoption as Draft African Regional Standards. Also, 15 Draft African Regional Standard Proposals on cement were prepared and sent to the ARSO Secretariat in 1984. The TC3 meeting, which was held from 7 to 14 November 1985 in Nairobi reviewed the work accomplished and studied the draft standard proposals presented by the secretariat. It then decided to adopt the 26 ISO standards presented as Draft African Regional Standards and the report on classification of building materials and components, leaving the standard proposals on low-cost housing to be studied in a detailed manner and to be presented later.

109. At present the TC3 has two standards on modular co-ordination and 28 Draft African Regional Standards (DARS). Out of these; one on modular co-ordination reference line of horizontal controlling dimensions has been withdrawn due to withdrawal by ISO, one is on building construction stairs vocabulary part 1, and one on joints in building vocabulary. The rest remaining 26 are on timber, wood and veneer plywood products and strengthening import-substitution strategies. The first meeting underlined the following building materials as priority items - bricks, tiles, cement, sandcrete blocks, concrete blocks and pipes, ceramics, lime, veneer plywood, particle board and fibre board, earth including sand and gravel, local stones, fibre reinforced cement, roofing sheets, reinforcement rods, glass, timber, sawn logs, furniture, bamboo, thatch, heat insulation materials, accoustical materials, gypsum, plastics and aluminium. Some of these materials have been already studied, and draft standard proposals have been prepared. Further studies will be conducted on the remaining materials.

79

PART IV

ESTABLISHMENT OF REGIONAL DATA BASES AND A PROGRAMME OF

INFORMATION EXCHANGE ON INDIGENOUS BUILDING MATERIALS

BY

AFRICAN REGIONAL ORGANIZATION FOR STANDARDIZATION (ARSO)

110.   Most African countries are at the stage of organizing their information resources and are facing difficulties in collecting documents produced in their own territories or accessing information available in other countries. This is very true in the field of human settlements which covers broad areas of housing, building and construction, public services, community facilities, environment and natural resources, physical planning, transport etc. However, with regard to local building materials, information processing and exchange could be facilitated if adequate means could be mobilized and if African countries were ready to provide information required to build Regional Data Bases and thus form the basis for an information-exchange programme.

111.   The African Regional Organization for Standardization (ARSO) is setting up an ARSO Network of Documentation and Information Systems (ARSO-DISNET) on standards and related matters, linking ARSO member States with the ARSO Documentation and Information System (ARSO-DIS). ARSO-DISNET is a network for collecting, processing and exchanging information on standards and related subjects. The participating centres of ARSO-DISNET are documentation centres of National Standards Bodies of ARSO member States. For the benefit of ARSO member States, regional data bases on standards and related matters are being developed at ARSO Headquarters by the ARSO Documentation and Information System (ARSO-DIS). Information used to establish those data bases is supplied by documentation centres which are participating in ARSO-DISNET and documentation centres on standards in other African countries.

112.   An information-exchange programme in local building materials can be accommodated within the ARSO Network of Documentation and Information Systems (ARSO-DISNET) on standards and related matters. The National Information Centres on Standards in African countries can liaise with different national sources on human settlements, to identify and collect documents and information on local building materials and forward these to the regional focal point (ARSO-DIS) responsible for processing and disseminating information and documents to network users.

I.   INFORMATION USERS AND NEEDS

113. The majority of Africans cannot have access to expensive housing and other building facilities; hence, the need for the development of cheap local building materials to cater for the expanding needs of the population. Information on local building materials is scattered among various national, regional and international institutions. Information stored by regional and international information centres can easily be made available on request, but information produced locally is mostly inaccessible, either because it is not identified or because the originators prefer not to publicize it for fear of abusing confidentiality. But researchers on local building materials should be informed on what information already exists, in order not to duplicate efforts unnecessarily.

114. Users vary in accordance with their function, but the following main four groups of users can be identified:

    - Training institutions: Lecturers need up-to-date information in order to pass on relevant knowledge to their students. These lecturers are usually part-time researchers. -Researchers: Researchers need to keep themselves continuously informed of the latest developments in their field at the domestic and foreign levels., in order to avoid duplication of work and to enable them to speed up their experiments.

- Standards officers: They must have in hand the required information for developing suitable standards for the African building industry.

- Professionals of the building industry: They include works foremen, laboratory technicians, instructors, supervisors and manufacturers. The information needs of these professionals is closely related to their daily activity, and they are people responsible for direct implementation of the results of research and standards on local building materials;

- Decision-makers and financing institutions: They need information for the planning process and for the funding of projects.

115.   Whatever the types of users, they should have access to required information and documents as rapidly as possible, in order to fulfil their duties efficiently and profitably. For this reason, they need to know what information exists, in which form it exists and where and how to get it. Hence, they need operational mechanisms for collecting and processing information and a suitable exchange programme.

II.   ESTABLISHMENT OF REGIONAL DATA BASES

116. Objectives of the data bases should be:

- To process and store technical information on local building materials available in Africa;

- To process and store information on institutions engaged or interested in the development and use of local building materials;

- To disseminate the above information to users through bibliographies, directories, catalogues, diskettes and magnetic tapes.

117. The types of data base to be developed are:

- A bibliographic data base. This data base will identify and store information on documents dealing with local building materials and will give a bibliographic description of documents. Documents will cover standards, research reports, workshop proceedings etc. A sample list of data fields for the bibliographic data base is shown in annex 1.

- A product data base. This data base will be a full-text data base on types and specifications of local building materials from the African region. It will also include codes of relevant documents entered in the bibliographic data base. A sample list of data fields for the product data base is shown in annex 2.

- A data base on institutions dealing with local building materials. This data base will give full addresses and details on activities of institutions engaged or interested in local building materials. These institutions include research organizations, standards bodies, financing institutions and companies manufacturing local building materials in Africa. A sample list of data fields for the data base on institutions is shown in annex 3.

- A data base on current projects on local building materials. This data base will describe research and standardization projects on local building materials. A sample list of data fields for the data base on projects is shown in annex 4.

III.   AN AFRICAN PROGRAMME ON INFORMATION COLLECTION, PROCESSING AND EXCHANGE

118.   One of the main constraints for information users is the lack of awareness of relevant information sources.   Thus, they need a programme which will cater for their information needs, by improving and systematizing the process of collection, processing and dissemination of information. A network will enable information centres in varying development stages and capabilities to put their resources together and share their human, material and technical potentialities among network members.   Thus, what cannot be done by one centre on its own can be achieved through national, regional and international co-operation.

119.   The network will enable the documentation centres which are members of it to:

- Improve and expand their activities, by ensuring the broad dissemination of the results of the work of their parent body and of national institutions;

- Gain access to regional data bases which will be constantly updating their records;

- Reduce the time devoted to the search for information;

- Avoid frequent duplication of activities.

If the networking approach is accepted by African countries, an information exchange programme could succeed.   Each member will be responsible for collecting and indexing documents from its own territory before forwarding them to ARSO.   The same methodology and common tools could be used by all network members. Information sent to ARSO by network members will be used for developing regional data bases.

120.   A national focal point should be identified in each African country to collect all relevant data on indigenous building

materials. This focal point should be a body related to the production of specifications and documents on local building materials. It should have qualified personnel and adequate facilities for storing and processing the required information. The national focal point could be the information centre of one of the following institutions: - Ministries of housing;

- National standards bodies;

- Research institutes on building materials;

- Professional associations on building activities;

- Institutions of learning in housing.

The national focal point should integrate its activities with those of the national subnetworks for collection and dissemination of information.

121.   Since the information exchange programme will concern African countries, it is necessary to identify a regional focal point which will play the role of co-ordinating centre and act as an information centre responsible for the establishment of Regional Data Bases on Indigenous Building Materials. This regional focal point should be hosted by ARSO and accommodated in the ARSO Documentation and Information System (ARSO-DIS). The role of the regional focal point can be:

- To collect primary documents on local building materials and   make them available to users;

- To orient users towards relevant information sources;

- To ensure the collection and processing of documents by the national focal points and the forwarding of these documents to ARSO-DIS;

- To give to network participants adequate common tools and methodology for collecting, processing and disseminating information;

- To develop regional data bases on activities on local building materials in Africa;

- To prepare product information to be disseminated to users on a regular basis or on request; and

- To promote the use of the network for getting information on local building materials in Africa.

122. The United Nations Centre for Human Settlements (Habitat) has achieved success in developing information on building materials and research projects in the field of human settlements. It has also developed thesauri and manuals which can be used by national focal points and the regional focal point to enable them to use a standardized language and common tools for processing information in the field of indigenous building materials. Its documentary products include:

- A bibliography on local building materials, plant and equipment, published in 1982;

- HABIRES: on going research data base in the field of human settlements published in 1986 and updated in 1987;

- Information sources on building and construction;

- Information sources on housing.

123. The common tools developed by UNCHS (Habitat) include:

- A thesaurus on human settlements terms and activities;

- A manual for librarians working in human settlements activities;

- Guidelines for Bibliographic Description and Abstracting of Human Settlements Literature.

124. UNCHS (Habitat) has also produced, the following directories to guide users to the appropriate institutions on human settlements in developing countries:

88

- Directory of National Research Organizations in Construction Materials and Technologies in Developing Countries;

- Directory of Information and Documentation Centres in the Field of Human Settlements in Developing Countries;

- Directory of Ministries and Governmental Institutions in the Field of Human Settlements in Developing Countries;

- Directory of Training Institutions in the Field of Human Settlements.

IV. CONCLUSION

125. The networking approach is the most suitable way to get hold of useful information on indigenous building materials in African countries and to disseminate the information appropriately. However, collection, processing and exchange of information can only succeed if each member of the network is fully committed to supplying information from its territory according to the rules and regulations of the network. UNCHS (Habitat) and ARSO should collaborate in the establishment of regional data bases and a programme on information exchange on indigenous building materials in Africa.

Annex 1:

MAIN DATA FIELDS OF THE BIBLIOGRAPHIC DATA BASE

1. Document identifier

2. Author

3. Status of document

4. Validity areas

5. Title in English

6. Title in French

7. Language of text

8. Supplier of document

9. Edition identifier and date of issue

10. Collation

11. Price

12. Abstract

13. Descriptors in English

14. Descriptors in French

15. Notes

Annex 2:

MAIN DATA FIELDS OF THE PRODUCT DATA BASE

1. Name of material

2. Definition

3. Main characteristics

4. Test methods

5. Certification mark

6. Certification system

7. Admission and control procedures for the product

8. Address of certification body

9. Addresses of manufacturers

10. Codes of documents related to the product and referred to in the bibliographic data base

11. Notes

Annex 3:

MAIN DATA FIELDS OF THE DATA BASE ON INSTITUTIONS

1. Name of institution

2. Address

3. Creation date

4. Name and position of contact person

5. Type of organization

6. Activities

7. Personnel

8. Budget

9. Information resource (types of services offered)

10. Codes of documents published by the institution and referred to
    in the bibliographic data base.

11. Notes

MAIN DATA FIELDS OF THE DATA BASE ON CURRENT PROJECTS

1. Institution's name and address

2. Project's field(s)

3. Title

4. Objectives

5. Descriptors

6. Status

7. Language

8. Leader(s) and technical personnel

9. Sponsor

10. Budget

11. Codes of documents published in the framework of the project and referred to in the bibliographic data base

12. Notes

Diagram showing information exchange arrangements in the Network.

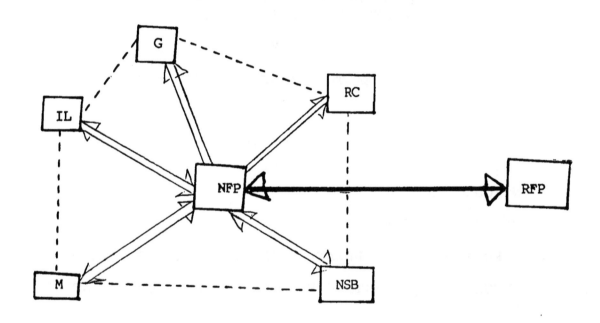

NFP   National Focal Point for information on indigenous building
        materials
RC   Research Centres
NSB   National Standards Bodies
G   Government departments
M   Manufacturers
IL   Institutions of Learning
RFP   The Regional Focal Point (ARSO-DIS) and its data bases
===⊳   Collection and dissemination of information at the national
        level
----   National cooperation arrangements
⟹   Exchange of information between National Focal Points and
        ARSO-DIS

Part V

RESEARCH AND DEVELOPMENT IN THE PROMOTION OF STANDARDS AND SPECIFICATIONS

BY

COMMONWEALTH SCIENCE COUNCIL (CSC)

CONTENTS   PAGE

INTRODUCTION

126. The Commonwealth Science Council's experience in the field of construction and building materials started with the project on Transfer of Rural Technology to Villages, established in 1978 as part of the Commonwealth Science Council's Co-ordinated Research and Development Programmes. 1/ The project, which terminated in 1983, essentially involved the transfer of housing technology to villages, based on the results of research findings from surveys of materials and housing designs in the traditional and/or low-cost shelter sector.

In its report entitled "Science and Technology for Development" the Expert Group on An Expanded Programme of Scientific Co-operation in the Commonwealth recommended, that the Commonwealth Science Council undertake collaborative research in the use of local construction and building materials as a means of enhancing both economic productivity and scientific capability. 2/ The project on Local Raw Materials and Technology for Housing Construction was subsequently launched, in June 1985, with the specific objective of promoting use of improved housing designs and selected local building materials for housing construction, notably for roofs, walls and foundations 3/

127. The current initiatives of Commonwealth Science Council are listed on Data Sheet 1 (appended). The project on Local Materials for Housing Construction (Africa) is a research and development collaboration with participation of Commonwealth member countries of the African region. Data Sheet 2 shows proposed areas of research and development by the various countries, following completion of Phase I of the Project (Surveys).

128. Commonwealth Science Council's interest in standards and standards-related issues in the African region dates from 1978,

when the Council established the African Programme on Standards and Quality Control (APSQC). The Programme has, since 1 January 1984, been transferred to the African Regional Organization for Standardization (ARSO) under a memorandum of understanding. The present paper outlines: (a) the Commonwealth Science Council's roles in the enhancement and promotion of policy-related efforts pertinent to the use of local building materials; (b) the Commonwealth Science Council's perspective on building materials and local building standards vis a vis the need for international co-operation in research and development; (c) the Common weath Science Council's proposal to establish a Network on Information Flow on Local Building Materials.

I. POLICY-RELATED EFFORTS١

129. With regard to the enhancement and promotion of policies pertinent to the use of local building materials, the Commonwealth Science Council has been adopting an indirect approach. It has recognized that national governments are the single largest clients of the building industry and so it has been urging member governments to promote the development of local building materials by:

(a) Utilizing local materials in selected government-sponsored projects;

(b) Encouraging the popular use of and quality production of local building materials, through the revision of existing regulatory procedures or the formulation of new codes, regulations, standards, specifications and other regulatory mechanisms in the building materials industry;

(c) Providing support to financial institutions so as to facilitate the availability of credit and capital for wide production and utilization of local building materials.

(d) Setting up or strengthening building research units or similar institutes;

(e) Establishing building research extension services in the rural areas for effective field trials and demonstrations. 4/

II.   INTERNATIONAL CO-OPERATION IN RESEARCH AND DEVELOPMENT

130.   In a majority of Commonwealth countries, existing building regulations, codes and statutory requirements are either outmoded or irrelevant. More often than not, they tend to make reference only to stardands of imported building materials and specifications. It is essential that available or potential building and construction procedures be able to provide housing, within the affordability of low-income groups. Thus this calls for:

(a) Predominant use of locally available raw materials for production of building materials and, subsequently, for housing construction;

(b) Promotion of appropriate standards. Commonwealth member countries should individually and severally gather as much information as possible to facilitate the formulation of or minimum standards.

131.   The Commonwealth Science Council's Local Raw Materials Project (Africa) has focused on regional research and collaboration of scientists from National Materials Research Institutions and related institutions. The Commonwealth Science Council is providing 'seed' funds to enable associated networks to attain a threshold momentum. The focus is on collaborative research and development, with technology transfer expected after successful demonstrations pertinent to materials production and shelter built-form design and construction have been achieved.

III. NETWORK ON INFORMATION FLOW ON LOCAL BUILDING MATERIALS (AFRICA)

132. To date the Commonwealth Science Council's _modus operandi_ on information dissemination has simply involved distribution to network scientists, collaborating institutions (national building research institutions, national standards institutions, national ministries of housing etc.) of publications arising from relevant workshops, commissioned studies, surveys and associated activities. It is Commonwealth Science Council's contention that a more systematic information acquisition, storage and dissemination mechanism could be realized with international collaboration. Documentation related to building materials for housing construction in a majority of countries of the African region is hardly ever available and even if available not easily accessible to those in need. The availability of relevant technical data and information including proven results of local research and development is a prerequisite for the formulation of realistic standards and specifications on a national regional or international basis. Therefore, the Network on Information Flow on Local Building Materials (Africa) has the following objectives:

(a) To establish a regional data base and a programme of information exchange on indigenous building materials in the region;

(b) To facilitate the acquisition, processing, storage, dissemination and exchange of information on indigenous building materials in the region;

(c) To assist in the strengthening of documentation capability of relevant national institutions (national building research institutions, national materials research institutions, national standards institutions, etc) in the area of indigenous building materials.

133.   To realize such a network will require extensive international operation involving:

(a) The support of international funding agencies;

(b) The support of international organisations with specialised interest in building materials;

(c) The support of relevant national institutions of the participating countries.

It is proposed that ARSO-CSC-UNCHS workshop on standards and specifications for local building materials considers the possibility of establishing such a network, deliberating, among others, over the mechanisms of implementation and continued sustainable co-operation in the network.

REFERENCES

1.   CSC(78)RT-1: Report on the Regional (Asia-Pacific) Workshop on Rural Technology, 18-25 January 1978, Dhaka, Bangladesh

2.   Science and Technology for Development: Report of the Expert Group on An Expanded Programme fo Scientific Co-operation in the Commonwealth, Commonwealth Science Council, London (1984)

3.   CSC(87)ISP-22: CSC Technical Series No. 215: Local Raw Materials for Housing Council, London (1987)

4.   CSC/85/58: Circular to Members of the Commonwealth Science Council in Africa on Summary of Recommendations of Workshop on the Use of Local Raw Materials for Construction, 17-21 June 1985, Kampala, Uganda.

LOCAL RAW MATERIALS FOR HOUSING CONSTRUCTION (AFRICA) CASE PROJECTION OF A CURRENT BUILDING MATERIALS PROJECT

1. General

1.1 Geographical location: Regional Commonwealth Africa

1.2 Physical context: Rural and suburban

1.3 Dates:

Phase		Commencement	Completion
Launch		June 1985	
I.	Surveys (Workshop on standards	June 1986	Dec-March 1987
	and specifications)	March-June 1987	March-June 1988
II.	Materials characterization (study visits)	March-June 1987	March-June 1988
III.	Performance characteristics studies (mid-term Workshop)	March-June 1987 March 1988	March-June 1988
IV.	Demonstration and field testing (study visits)	June-Sept 1988 -	June-Sept 1989 -
V.	Evaluation (end-term workshop)	Sept-Dec 1989 -	- -

1.4 Beneficiaries: Rural and suburban people the low-cost housing sector.

2. Project purpose

2.1 Background:

The need to provide a forum for co-operative research and development in the field of local building materials for housing construction was realised at a regional Commonwealth (Africa) workshop/seminar on the Use of Local Raw Materials for Construction held in Kampala, Uganda, 17-21 June 1985, which recommended the establishment of the above project. The project was recognized and endorsed by the 18th Executive Meeting of Commonwealth Science Council in London, July 1985.

2.2   Project Objectives:

2.2.1   General

    To enhance scientific capability (including design skills) that is responsive to:

-   the identification, selection, design and development of local raw materials for housing construction;

-   the development of durable and cost-effective housing design using local raw materials.

2.2.2   Specific

To realize improved housing design and improved functionality and performance of local raw materials that are viable for local housing construction in the areas of roofing, walling and foundation.

2.2.3   Mechanism

To realize the above objectives by collaborative endeavours pertinent to local raw materials and construction designs, particularly for low- cost housing, and involving surveys, commissioned studies and setting up of demonstration units.

2.3   Project scope:

    Component I: Pozzolanic materials
                    Development of pozzolanic materials as partial

    Component II: Utilization of soils and building stones
                    for low-cost housing

    Component III: Properties of wood
                    Study of wood and its properties for housing
                    construction

    Component IV: Design engineering
                    Development of improved construction designs
                    in low-cost housing, using local raw
                    materials

2.4 Related initiatives:

2.4.1 Formulation of standards and specifications for selected local building materials, viz, adobe, burnt-clay, bricks, stabilized soil bricks, lime, pozzolanas and fibre-based roofing sheets in the framework of the ARSO/CSC/UNCHS workshop on standards and specifications for local building materials.

2.4.2 Assistance by Commonwealth Secretariat's Industrial Development Unit (IDU) to several Commonwealth countries in the identification and establishment of industries in the building materials/housing construction sector, mainly small-scale industries. The scope of building materials industries to be assisted will cover burnt-clay bricks and tiles, cement, timber and lime.

2.4.3 Commonwealth Science Council's project on Passive Solar Architecture, initiated in the Caribbean, is envisaged to be extended to the African region.

3. Project participation

3.1 Sponsoring organization: CSC

sponsoring of workshops, surveys, commissioned studies, study visits and demonstration units, systematic co-ordination.

3.2 End-users:

Part participation in surveys and setting up of demonstration units.

3.3 Network scientists:

Local implementation of surveys, commissioned studies and demonstration units.

3.4 Collaborating agencies:

Commonwealth Science Council/Commonwealth Fund for Technical co-operation, UNCHS, ARSO, UNIDO, ITDG.

4. Project outcome

The project is expected to realize the following outputs:

- Local building materials (for low-cost housing) with improved performance characteristics;

- Local built-form designs (for low-cost housing) with improved performance characteristics;

- Set of recommendations (standards, specifications, etc). on selected local building materials, including adobe, burnt-clay bricks, stabilized-soil bricks, lime and pozzolana.

PART VI

STANDARDS AND SPECIFICATIONS: AN INTEGRATED APPROACH TO THE DEVELOPMENT

OF LOCAL BUILDING MATERIALS FOR LOW-COST HOUSING

BY

UNITED NATIONS ECONOMIC COMMISSION FOR AFRICA (ECA)

INTRODUCTION

134.   The recent economic crisis heightened by widespread famine and desertification which have plagued the African continent, has highlighted the plight of the people and their living conditions.   It has revealed the fragility of organizational and physical infrastructure, the neglect of the rural hinterland and the isolation of the rural community from the mainstream of the development process.   This, coupled with rising building costs and decreasing purchasing power, has worsened the shelter situation in African countries.

135.   However, in conformity with Africa's Priority Programme for Economic Recovery and the deliberations of the Joint Intergovernmental Regional Committee on Human Settlements and Environment for Africa, Member States have resolved to promote rural transformation and development of the building materials and construction industries.   The aim is to improve lifestyles in the rural areas and increase food production.   To revitalize the rural hinterland would require low-cost solutions for the provision of shelter and infrastructures and self-reliance in the construction sector.   As long as Africa is dependent on imported factor inputs, rural transformation will not be realized.   It is, therefore, imperative to emphasize the development and utilization of indigenous building materials and local skills.

136.   The commitment of Governments of Member States to channel resources to the rural hinterland would need a very judicious programme of action, particularly in the development of the building materials industry.   Standards and specifications should not be too rigid, in order to avoid inhibiting production and utilization.   Yet, investment would require some form of assurance of safety and durability of the materials used.   The ECA programme is concerned with promoting durable locally

produced materials. This approach relies on production methods and quality control rather than on testing procedures which may prove over-ambitious in application, particularly in rural areas.

I. REALISTIC AND AFFORDABLE PROCEDURES

137. While the programme sees the merit of developing suitable standards for local building materials, ECA is mindful that procedures for achieving and verifying these standards and specifications should not inhibit the production of local materials. Small-scale informal units constitute the mainstay of the ECA programme for the production of local building materials. While their level of know-how investment cannot be expected to support complex scientific standard testing procedures, they are and will continue to be relied upon for the production of local building materials. The ECA programme therefore, emphasizes the need for improved production methods and quality control at the production stage.

II. TARGET GROUP

138. The ECA programme is designed to promote the construction of low-income housing, and standards and specifications should not be viewed as an end in themselves but rather as a means of promoting standards-quality materials. It would, therefore, be worth developing simplified testing procedures which would provide a framework for improved production capabilities. However, the ECA programme at this stage of development views standards and specifications as guidelines and not necessarily rigid norms.

III PROMOTION OF LOCAL BUILDING MATERIALS

139.   The primary function of the ECA programme at this stage of development is to promote the production and utilization of local building materials through the existing network of production facilities.   The ECA programme aims at expanding existing production - capabilities while improving the quality of materials produced by offering more incentives to entrepreneurs and users.   Standards and specifications which might evolve should ensure consistency and durability of the materials at affordable market prices.

140.   The programme also relies on research and development institutions in the African region for achieving its programme objectives.   Most of these research and development institutions have been engaged in the development of local building materials for some time.   It is, therefore, expected that these research and development institutions will contribute actively to the regional programme, by developing production methods and practices   which will   attract entrepreneurs and financial institutions to invest venture capital in the production of local materials for low-cost housing.   Under this programme, the research and development institutions will qualify for direct financial contributions for mobilizing technical, material and logistic support.

141.   The programme will foster co-operation and exchange of information on the production of materials between research and development institutions.   In addition, the programme will endeavour to identify and disseminate, in Africa, research findings and production practices in specific materials from outside the region.   Entrepreneurs will work in close collaboration with both research and development and financial

institutions in the region, in order to promote scientifically and financially acceptable projects.

IV. DEMONSTRATION PROJECT

142. The regional programme will have a positive impact on the housing sector, if Governments of Member States and regional and international financial institutions will initiate the construction of low-cost housing demonstration schemes utilizing local materials. Such schemes will generate confidence in entrepreneurs and the public at large for the utilization of local building materials. Accordingly, ECA, with the active support of Shelter-Afrique and UNCHS (Habitat), is studying means of mobilizing resources for constructing demonstration low-cost housing schemes and promoting the establishment of commercial small-scale production units.

V. RECOMMENDATIONS

143. The ECA programme recognizes the need for appropriate standards and specifications in the development of local building materials. Application must consider the following:

(a) Standards and specifications should not impede the production and utilization of local materials for low-cost housing;

(b) The stage of development of the African region should be borne in mind before rigid regulatory instruments are proposed for enforcement;

(c) The consumer should be protected by means of dissemination of information and promotion of good production practice;

(d) Standards and specifications should be developed at research and development institutions as a means of promoting

www.ingramcontent.com/pod-product-compliance
Lightning Source LLC
Jackson TN
JSHW050539141224
75386JS00038B/1275